YOU HAVE AT YOUR COMMAND . . .

a supercomputer with a memory bank that surpasses any other kind of computer on earth. This marvelous piece of equipment is your brain. Everything you have ever seen and heard is stored there, waiting to be called into consciousness. And now at last you have a way to instantly tap your perfect memory whenever you want to use it.

In USE YOUR PERFECT MEMORY, Tony Buzan, world-famous authority on the brain and the learning process, combines ancient wisdom and new Mind Mapping methods in a remarkable step-by-step program. Just as there is virtually no limit to your memory, there is no limit to the uses of this marvelous guide. Whether you are a business person or student, young or old, this is the book to remember if you want to remember everything else.

TONY BUZAN is one of the world's leading authorities on the brain and learning techniques. His training companies advise top- and middle-management executives of such corporations as IBM and Mobil. In addition, several television programs have been created around his learning techniques, among them the famed ten-part BBC series "Use Your head," the basis for his global bestseller, *Use Both Sides of Your Brain*.

ALSO BY TONY BUZAN

Books

Use Both Sides of Your Brain
Master Your Memory
Speed Reading
Memory Visions (workbook for *Master Your Memory*)
The Brain User's Guide
Make the Most of Your Mind
Harnessing the ParaBrain
   (Business version of *Make the Most of Your Mind*)
Spore One (poetry – limited edition)

Videotapes

Use Both Sides of Your Brain
The Enchanted Loom
Buzan Business Training
Family Genius Training

Audiotapes

Learning and Memory
The Intelligence Revolution
Make the Most of Your Mind
Supercreativity and Mind Mapping

Other works

The Universal Personal Organiser
'Body and Soul' (Master Mind Map poster)
The Mind Map Kit
Master Your Memory Matrix (SEM^3) 0–10,000
The Brain Club Manifesto
The Brain Club Magazine

see *Appendix* for more information, including how to order these items

THIRD EDITION

USE YOUR PERFECT MEMORY

Dramatic new techniques for improving your memory—based on the latest discoveries about the human brain

TONY BUZAN

COMPLETELY REVISED AND UPDATED

A PLUME BOOK

To Zeus and Mnemosyne's ideal muse-child:
my dear, dear friend Lorraine Gill, the Artist

External Editor-in-chief: Vanda North

With thanks to all those whose effort and co-operation enabled me to write
this book:

Zita Albes; Jennie Allen; Astrid Andersen; Jeannie Beattie; Nick Beytes; Mark
Brown; Joy Buttery; my brother, Barry Buzan; Bernard Chibnall; Carol Coaker;
Steve and Fanny Colling; Susan Crockford; Tricia Date; Janet Dominey; Charles
Elton; Janice English; Lorraine Gill; Bill Harris; Brian Helweg-Larsen; Thomas
Jarlov; Trish Lillis; Hermione Lovell; Annette McGee; Joe McMahon; Vanda
North; Khalid Ranjah; Pep Reiff; Auriol Roberts; Ian Rosenbloom; Caitrina Ni
Shuilleabhain; Robert Millard Smith; Chris and Pat Stevens; Jan Streit;
Christopher Tatham; Lee Taylor; Nancy Thomas; Sue Vaudin; Jim Ward; Bill
Watts; Gillian Watts; Phyllida Wilson.

PLUME
Published by the Penguin Group
Penguin Books USA Inc., 375 Hudson Street, New York, New York 10014, U.S.A.
Penguin Books Ltd, 27 Wrights Lane, London W8 5TZ, England
Penguin Books Australia Ltd, Ringwood, Victoria, Australia
Penguin Books Canada Ltd, 10 Alcorn Ave., Suite 300, Toronto, Canada M4V
3B2
Penguin Books (N.Z.) Ltd, 182-190 Wairau Road, Auckland 10, New Zealand
Penguin Books Ltd, Registered Offices: Harmondsworth, Middlesex, England

Published by Plume, an imprint of New American Library, a division of Penguin
Books USA Inc. Simultaneously published in a Dutton hardcover edition.

First Plume Printing, January, 1991
30 29 28 27 26

REGISTERED TRADEMARK—MARCA REGISTRADA

LIBRARY OF CONGRESS CATALOGING-IN-PUBLICATION DATA

Buzan, Tony.
    Use your perfect memory / Tony Buzan — [3rd ed.]
        p.   cm.
    Includes bibliographical references.
    ISBN 0-452-26606-8
    1. Mnemonics. I. Title.
BF391.B88   1991b
153.1'4—dc20
                                                            90-10571
                                                            CIP
Printed in the United States of America

Contents

Introduction

Like so many children, as a youth I was mystified by the wonderful and elusive faculty called memory. In casual and relaxed situations it worked so smoothly that I hardly ever noticed it; in examinations it only occasionally performed well, to my surprise, but was more often associated with 'bad memory', the fearful area of forgetting. Since I spent much of my childhood in the country with animals, I began to realise that the misnamed 'dumb' creatures seemed to have extraordinary memories, often superior to my own. Why, then, was human memory apparently so faulty?

I began to study in earnest, eagerly devouring information about how the early Greeks had devised specific memory systems for various tasks; and how later, the Romans applied these techniques to enable themselves to remember whole books of mythology and to impress their audiences during senatorial speeches and debates. My interest became more focused while I was in college, when the realisation slowly dawned on me that such basic systems need not be used only for 'rote' or parrotlike memory, but could be used as gigantic filing systems for the mind, enabling extraordinarily fast and efficient access, and enormously enhancing general understanding. I applied the techniques in taking examinations, in playing games with my imagination in order to improve my memory, and in helping other students, who were supposedly on the road to academic failure, achieve first-class successes.

The explosion of brain research during the last decade has confirmed what the memory theorists, gamesters, mnemonic technicians and magicians have always known: that the holding capacity of our brains and the ability to recall what is stored there are far and deliciously beyond normal expectations.

Use Your Perfect Memory, a major new development from the memory sections of *Use Both Sides of Your Brain,* is an initial tour through what should have been included as first among the seven wonders of the world: the 'hanging gardens' of your limitless memory and imagination.

How to use
Use Your Perfect Memory

Use Your Perfect Memory has been designed to enable you to achieve your memory goals as rapidly as possible.

It is divided into three main parts: Part I covers Memory History and Systems; Part II the Major System and its Application to Memory; and Part III the uses of Mind Maps for Memorising.

More specifically, chapters 1 to 9 provide you with a check of your current memory capabilities, with background information on your memory, including the foundations and principles you will require for developing a superpower memory. The first basic link and list systems for memorising 10, 20 and 26 items, are explained.

Chapter 10 then shows you how to multiply any system you have learnt by first a factor of ten, and then by a factor of ten again!

Chapter 11 introduces you to your memory's rhythms over time, enabling you to manage yourself and life in such a way as to increasingly enhance your memory's functioning.

Chapter 12 introduces you to the Major System. This system is so named because it forms the basis for a limitless series of other memory systems, and can be specifically applied to the memorisation of those areas dealt with in chapters 14 to 21: the memorisation of cards; the development of your IQ through long number memory; telephone numbers; schedules and appointments; dates in the current century; historical dates; birthdays and anniversaries; and vocabulary and language learning.

Chapter 22 introduces you to the new technique of Mind Mapping, an approach to the art of memory that will allow you to note and record in a manner that will improve your retention and recall by as much as 10 times the average.

The Mind Mapping technique can be applied, with other memory systems and approaches, to the next five chapters (23 to 27) on the memorisation of names and faces, the recalling of things you thought you had forgotten, the writing and passing of examinations, the giving of speeches and telling of jokes, and the recalling of your dreams.

It is recommended that you browse through the whole book first, then complete chapters 1 to 13 to give yourself a solid foundation.

Having reached this stage, you may either continue through the book on a chapter-by-chapter basis, choosing any chapter from 14 to 21, or jump ahead to chapter 22 and subsequently pick your preferred choices from chapters 23 to 28.

Above all, make sure that as you progress through the book you use, to their fullest extent, your **associative** and **imaginative** abilities, and that you enjoy yourself!

PART I: MEMORY — ITS HISTORY AND SYSTEMS

1 Is your memory perfect?

Your memory is phenomenal. This statement is made despite the following counterarguments:

1 Most people remember fewer than 10 per cent of the names of those whom they meet.
2 Most people forget more than 99 per cent of the phone numbers given to them.
3 Memory is supposed to decline rapidly with age.
4 Many people drink, and alcohol is reputed to destroy 1000 brain cells per drink.
5 Internationally, across races, cultures, ages and education levels, there is a common experience, and fear of, having an inadequate or bad memory.
6 Our failures in general, and especially in remembering, are attributed to the fact that we are 'only human', a statement that implies that our skills are inherently inadequate.
7 You will probably fail most of the memory tests in the following chapter.

Points 1, 2 and 7 will be dealt with through the remainder of the book. You will see that it is possible, with appropriate knowledge, to pass all the tests, and that names and phone numbers are easy to remember – if you know how.

Your memory may decline with age, but only if it is not used. Conversely, if it is used, it will continue to improve throughout your lifetime.

There is no evidence to suggest that moderate drinking destroys brain cells. This misapprehension arose because it was found that excessive drinking, and only excessive drinking, did indeed damage the brain.

Across cultural and international boundaries 'negative experience' with memory can be traced not to our being 'only human' or in any way innately inadequate but to two simple, easily changeable factors: (1) negative mental set and (2) lack of knowledge.

NEGATIVE MENTAL SET

There is a growing and informal international organisation, which I choose to name the 'I've Got an Increasingly Bad Memory Club'. How often do you hear people in animated and enthusiastic conversation saying things like, 'You know, my memory's not nearly as good as it used to be when I was younger; I'm constantly forgetting things.' To which there is an equally enthusiastic reply: 'Yes, I know exactly what you mean; the same thing's happening to me. . . .' And off they dodder, arms draped around each other's shoulders, down the hill to mental oblivion. And such conversations often take place between 30-year-olds!

This negative, dangerous, *incorrect* mental set is based on lack of proper training, and this book is designed to correct it.

Consider the younger supermemoriser to whom most people romantically refer. If you want to check for yourself, go back to any school at the end of the day, walk into a classroom of a group of five to seven-year-old children after they have gone home and ask the teacher what has been left in the classroom (i.e. forgotten). You will find the following items: watches, pencils, pens, sweets, money, jackets, physical education equipment, books, coats, glasses, erasers, toys, etc.

The only real difference between the middle-aged executive who has forgotten to phone someone he was supposed to phone and who has left his briefcase at the office, and the seven-year-old child who realises on returning home that he's left at school his watch, his pocket-money and his homework is that the seven-year-old does not collapse into depression, clutching his head and exclaiming, 'Oh God, I'm seven years old and my memory's going!'

Ask yourself, 'What is the number of things I actually remember each day?' Most people estimate somewhere between 100 and 10,000. The answer is in fact in the multiple billions. The human memory is so excellent and runs so smoothly that most people don't even realise that every word they speak and every word they listen to are instantaneously produced for consideration, recalled, recognised precisely and placed in their appropriate context. Nor do they realise that every moment, every perception, every thought, *everything* that they do throughout the entire day and throughout their lives is a function of their memories. In fact, its ongoing accuracy is almost perfect. The few odd things that we do forget are like odd specks on a gigantic ocean. Ironically, the reason why we notice so dramatically the errors that we make is that they are so rare.

There is now increasing evidence that our memories may not only be far better than we ever thought but may in fact be perfect. Consider the following arguments for this case:

1 Dreams

Many people have vivid dreams of acquaintances, friends, family and lovers of whom they have not thought for as many as 20 to 40 years. In their dreams, however, the images are *perfectly* clear, all colours and details being exactly as they were in real life. This confirms that somewhere in the brain there is a vast store of perfect images and associations that does not change with time and that, with the right trigger, can be recalled. In chapter 26 you will learn about Catching Your Dreams.

2 Surprise Random Recall

Practically everyone has had the experience of turning a corner and suddenly recalling people or events from previous times in his life. This often happens when people revisit their first school. A single smell, touch, sight or sound can bring back a flood of experiences thought to be forgotten. This ability of any given sense to reproduce perfect memory images, the fact that the smell of bread baking or the sound of a song can bathe your mind in the past, indicates that if there were more correct 'trigger situations' much more would and could be recollected. We know from such experiences that the brain has retained the information.

3 The Russian 'S' (Shereshevsky)

In the early part of this century a young Russian journalist, Shereshevsky (in *The Mind of a Mnemonist*, by A. R. Luria, he is referred to as 'S') attended an editorial meeting, and it was noted to the consternation of others that he was not taking notes. When pressed to explain, he became confused; to everyone's amazement, it became apparent that he really did not understand why anyone should ever take notes. The explanation that he gave for not taking notes himself was that he could remember what the editor was saying, so what was the point? Upon being challenged, 'S' reproduced the entire speech, word for word, sentence for sentence, and inflection for inflection. For the next 30 years he was to be tested and examined by Alexander Luria, Russia's leading psychologist and expert on memory. Luria confirmed that 'S' was in no way abnormal but that his memory was indeed perfect. Luria also stated that at a very young age 'S' had 'stumbled upon' the basic mnemonic principles (see pages 41ff.) and that they had become part of his natural functioning.

'S' was not unique. The history of education, medicine and psychology is dotted with similar cases of perfect memorisers. In every instance, their brains were found to be normal, and in every instance they had, as young children, 'discovered' the basic principles of their memory's function.

4 Professor Rosensweig's Experiments

Professor Mark Rosensweig, a Californian psychologist and neuro-physiologist, spent years studying the individual brain cell and its capacity for storage. As early as 1974 he stated that if we fed in ten new items of information *every second* for an entire lifetime to any normal human brain that brain would be considerably less than half full. He emphasised that memory problems have nothing to do with the capacity of the brain but rather with the self-management of that apparently limitless capacity.

5 Professor Penfield's Experiments

Professor Wilder Penfield of Canada came across his discovery of the capacity of human memory by mistake. He was stimulating indi-vidual brain cells with tiny electrodes for the purpose of locating areas of the brain that were the cause of patients' epilepsy.

To his amazement he found that when he stimulated certain indi-vidual brain cells, his patients were suddenly recalling experiences from their past. The patients emphasised that it was not simple memory, but that they actually were reliving the entire experience, including smells, noises, colours, movement, tastes. These experi-ences ranged from a few hours before the experimental session to as much as 40 years earlier.

Penfield suggested that hidden within each brain cell or cluster of brain cells lies a perfect store of every event of our past and that if we could find the right stimulus we could replay the entire film.

6 The Potential Pattern-Making Ability of Your Brain

Professor Pyotr Anokhin, the famous Pavlov's brightest student, spent his last years investigating the potential pattern-making capabilities of the human brain. His findings were important for memory researchers. It seems that memory is recorded in separate little patterns, or electromagnetic circuits, that are formed by the brain's interconnecting cells.

Anokhin already knew that the brain contained a million million (1,000,000,000,000) brain cells but that even this gigantic number was going to be small in comparison with the number of patterns that those brain cells could make among themselves. Working with advanced electron microscopes and computers, he came up with a staggering number. Anokhin calculated that the number of patterns, or 'degrees of freedom', throughout the brain is, to use his own words, 'so great that writing it would take a line of figures, in normal manuscript characters, more than ten and a half million *kilometres* in

length. With such a number of possibilities, the brain is a keyboard on which hundreds of millions of different melodies can be played.'
Your memory is the music.

7 Near-Death-Type Experiences

Many people have looked up at the surface ripples of a swimming pool from the bottom, knowing that they were going to drown within the next two minutes; or seen the rapidly disappearing ledge of the mountain from which they have just fallen; or felt the oncoming grid of the 10-ton lorry bearing down on them at 60 miles per hour. A common theme runs through the accounts that survivors of such traumas tell. In such moments of 'final consideration' the brain slows all things down to a standstill, expanding a fraction of a second into a lifetime, and reviews the *total* experience of the individual.

When pressed to admit that what they had really experienced were a few highlights, the individuals concerned insisted that what they had experienced was their *entire* life, including all things they had completely forgotten until that instant of time. 'My whole life flashed before me' has almost become a cliché that goes with the near-death experience. Such a commonality of experience again argues for a storage capacity of the brain that we have only just begun to tap.

8 Photographic Memory

Photographic, or eidetic, memory is a specific phenomenon in which people can remember, usually for a very short time, perfectly and exactly anything they have seen. This memory usually fades, but it can be so accurate as to enable somebody, after seeing a picture of 1000 randomly sprayed dots on a white sheet, to reproduce them perfectly. This suggests that in addition to the deep, long-term storage capacity, we also have a shorter-term and immediate photographic ability. It is argued that children often have this ability as a natural part of their mental functioning and that we train it away by forcing them to concentrate too much on logic and language and too little on imagination and their other range of mental skills.

9 The 1000 Photographs

In recent experiments people were shown 1000 photographs, one after the other, at a pace of about one photograph per second. The psychologists then mixed 100 photographs with the original 1000, and asked the people to select those they had not seen the first time through. Everyone, regardless of how he described his normal memory, was able to identify almost every photograph he had seen – as well as each one that he had not seen previously. They were not necessarily able to remember the order in which the photographs had been presented, but they could definitely remember the image – an example that confirms the common human experience of being better able to remember a face than the name attached to it. This particular problem is easily dealt with by applying the Memory Techniques.

10 The Memory Techniques

The Memory Techniques, or mnemonics, were a system of 'memory codes' that enabled people to remember perfectly whatever it was they wished to remember. Experiments with these techniques have shown that if a person scores 9 out of 10 when using such a technique, that same person will score 900 out of 1000, 9000 out of 10,000, 900,000 out of 1,000,000 and so on. Similarly, one who scores perfectly out of 10 will score perfectly out of 1,000,000. These techniques help us to delve into that phenomenal storage capacity we have and to pull out whatever it is that we need. The Memory Principles are outlined in chapter 4, and the bulk of this book is devoted to explaining and outlining the most important and useful of these systems, showing how easily they can be learned, and how they can be applied in personal, family, business and community life.

At this early stage, however, it should be helpful for you to test your memory in its current state. The following chapter provides a series of memory tests that will form a foundation from which you can check your progress. If you are interested in the truth about yourself and your performance now, as compared with what it will be when you have completed the book, perform these tests thoroughly. Most people do rather poorly at the beginning, improving dramatically as they progress through the chapters.

2 Checking your current memory capabilities

Few people ever put their memories to the immediate test, and it is for this reason that most are unaware of the false limits, the habits and potential of their minds. Because of the way we are trained (or not trained) in school, the simple tasks you will soon attempt will in some cases prove very difficult and in others almost impossible. Yet these tasks are perfectly within the capacity of the average human brain. Do not worry about poor performance, however, since it is the purpose of this book to make memorisation, such as is required in the following tests, an easy and enjoyable exercise.

LINK TEST

Read the following list of twenty items through *once* only, trying to memorise both the items and the order in which they are listed. Then turn to page 25 to test yourself and for scoring instructions.

Wallpaper	Elephant
Mountain	Jail
Skirt	Mirror
String	Suitcase
Ice cream	Plant
Scissors	Power
Nail	Safe
Watch	Melon
Nurse	Mongrel
Perfume	Engraving

PEG TEST

Give yourself sixty seconds to memorise the following list of 10 items. The aim in this test is to remember the items in random order, connecting them to their appropriate number. When your minute has passed, turn to page 25 and fill in the answers.

1 Atom	6 Tile
2 Tree	7 Windscreen
3 Stethoscope	8 Honey
4 Sofa	9 Brush
5 Alley	10 Toothpaste

NUMBER TEST

Look at the four 15-digit numbers printed below, giving not more than a half-minute to each. At the end of each half-minute section turn to page 26 and write down the number as best you can.

1 798465328185423   **3** 784319884385628

2 493875941254945   **4** 825496581198762

TELEPHONE NUMBER TEST

The following is a list of ten people and their telephone numbers. Study the list for not more than two minutes and attempt to remember all the phone numbers, then turn to page 26 and answer the appropriate questions.

Your health-food shop	787-5953
Your tennis partner	640-7336
Your local weather bureau	691-0262
Your local newsagent	242-9111
Your local florist	725-8397
Your local garage	781-3702
Your local theatre	869-9521
Your local discothèque	644-1616
Your local community centre	457-8910
Your favourite restaurant	354-6350

CARD TEST

This test is designed to exercise your present capacity in remembering cards and their sequence. The list below contains all 52 cards of the regular pack in numbered order. Your task is to spend not more than three minutes looking at this list, and then to recall it. Turn to page 27 to fill in your answers.

1	Ten of diamonds	**27**	Four of hearts
2	Ace of spades	**28**	Two of diamonds
3	Three of hearts	**29**	Jack of spades
4	Jack of clubs	**30**	Six of spades
5	Five of clubs	**31**	Two of hearts
6	Five of hearts	**32**	Four of diamonds
7	Six of hearts	**33**	Three of spades
8	Eight of clubs	**34**	Eight of diamonds
9	Ace of clubs	**35**	Ace of hearts
10	Queen of clubs	**36**	Queen of spades
11	King of spades	**37**	Queen of diamonds
12	Ten of hearts	**38**	Six of diamonds
13	Six of clubs	**39**	Nine of spades
14	Three of diamonds	**40**	Ten of clubs
15	Four of spades	**41**	King of hearts
16	Four of clubs	**42**	Nine of hearts
17	Queen of hearts	**43**	Eight of spades
18	Five of spades	**44**	Seven of spades
19	Jack of diamonds	**45**	Three of clubs
20	Seven of hearts	**46**	Ace of diamonds
21	Nine of clubs	**47**	Ten of spades
22	King of diamonds	**48**	Eight of hearts
23	Seven of clubs	**49**	Seven of diamonds
24	Two of spades	**50**	Nine of diamonds
25	Jack of hearts	**51**	Two of clubs
26	King of clubs	**52**	Five of diamonds

FACE TEST

Look at the ten faces on the following two pages for not more than two minutes, then turn to pages 28 and 29 where the same faces are present without their names. Try to match the right name to the right face. Scoring instructions are on page 29.

1 Mrs Whitehead

2 Mr Hawkins

3 Mr Fisher

4 Mr Ramm

5 Mrs Hemming

6 Mrs Briar

7 Mr Chester

8 Mr Master

9 Mrs Swanson

10 Miss Temple

DATES TEST

This is your last test: listed below are ten fairly important historical dates. Give yourself two minutes to remember them all perfectly, then turn to page 30.

1 1666 Great Fire of London
2 1770 Beethoven's birthday
3 1215 Signing of Magna Carta
4 1917 Russian Revolution
5 1454 First printing press
6 1815 Battle of Waterloo
7 1608 Invention of the telescope
8 1905 Einstein's Theory of Relativity
9 1789 French Revolution
10 1776 American Declaration of Independence

LINK TEST RESPONSE   (See p. 19)

Note in the space provided all the items you can remember, in correct order.

Score yourself in two ways: first enter below the number of items you remembered out of 20, and then record the number of items you listed in the correct order. (If you reversed two items, they are both wrong with regard to order.) Score one point for each remembered; one point for each correct placing (total possible: 40).

Number remembered: _____   Number incorrect: _____
Number in correct order: _____   Number in incorrect order: _____

PEG TEST RESPONSE   (See p. 20)

In the order indicated, place the item you were given next to its appropriate number.

10	1
8	3
6	5
4	7
2	9

Number correct: _____

NUMBER TEST RESPONSE (See p. 20)

In the space below write down each of the four 15-digit numbers.

1 _____

2 _____

3 _____

4 _____

Score one point for every digit that you record *in its proper sequence.*

Total score: ____
              60

TELEPHONE NUMBER TEST RESPONSE (See p. 20)

Write down, in the space provided, the phone numbers of the ten people.

Name	Number
1 Your health-food shop	_____
2 Your tennis partner	_____
3 Your local weather bureau	_____
4 Your local newsagent	_____
5 Your local florist	_____
6 Your local garage	_____
7 Your local theatre	_____
8 Your local discothèque	_____
9 Your local community centre	_____
10 Your favourite restaurant	_____

Scoring: give yourself one mark for each correct number (even if you make only one mistake in the number you must consider this totally wrong, for if you had dialled it you would not have been put in contact with the person with whom you wished to speak). The highest possible score is 10.

Score: ____
        10

CARD TEST RESPONSE (See p. 21)

Recall the list in reverse order (52–1) as indicated.

52	26
51	25
50	24
49	23
48	22
47	21
46	20
45	19
44	18
43	17
42	16
41	15
40	14
39	13
38	12
37	11
36	10
35	9
34	8
33	7
32	6
31	5
30	4
29	3
28	2
27	1

Score one point for each correct answer. A score of 52 is perfect.

FACE TEST RESPONSE (See pp. 22 and 23)

Fit the names to the faces:

8

7

6

1   5

3

2

9

4

10

Score one point for each correct answer.

DATES TEST RESPONSE (See p. 24)

9 _____ French Revolution

6 _____ Battle of Waterloo

1 _____ Great Fire of London

10 _____ American Declaration of Independence

2 _____ Beethoven's birthday

5 _____ First printing press

4 _____ Russian Revolution

3 _____ Signing of Magna Carta

8 _____ Einstein's Theory of Relativity

7 _____ Invention of the telescope

Scoring: give yourself one point for an accurate answer and half a point if you come within five years. Ten points is a perfect score.

Now calculate your total score for all the tests – perfect is 192.

TEST RESULT SUMMARY

Test	Your Score	Possible Total
Link Test		40
Peg Test		10
Number Test		60
Telephone Number Test		10
Card Test		52
Face Test		10
Dates Test		10
		192

To calculate Summary Per Cent Score:
Divide Your Score (YS) into the Possible Total $\left(\dfrac{PT}{YS} = x\right)$

Then divide the result (x) into 100 $\left(\dfrac{100}{x}\right)$

= Your Summary Per Cent Score

This completes your initial testing (there will be other tests for you to experiment with throughout the text). Normal scores on each of these tests range from 20 to 60 per cent. Even a score of 60 per cent, which in the average group will be considered excellent, is well below what you can expect of yourself when you have absorbed the information in this book. The average trained memoriser would have scored between 95 and 100 per cent on every one of the foregoing tests.

The next chapter outlines the history of memory, giving you a context in which to learn the memory techniques and systems, and shows how recently it is that we have begun to understand your amazing innate abilities.

3 The history of memory

From the time when man first began to depend on his mind for coping with his environment, the possession of an excellent memory has been a step to positions of command and respect. Throughout human history there have been recorded remarkable – sometimes legendary – feats of memory.

THE GREEKS

It is difficult to say exactly when and where the first integrated ideas on memory arose. The first sophisticated concepts, however, can be attributed to the Greeks, some 600 years before the birth of Christ. As we look back on them now, these 'sophisticated' ideas were surprisingly naïve, especially since some of the men proposing them are numbered among the greatest thinkers the world has ever known.

In the **sixth century BC**, Parmenides thought of memory as being a mixture of light and dark or heat and cold. He believed that as long as any given mixture remained unstirred, the memory would be perfect. As soon as the mixture was altered, forgetting occurred. Diogenes of Apollonia advanced a different theory, in the **fifth century BC**. He suggested that memory was a process that consisted of events producing an equal distribution of air in the body. Like Parmenides, he thought that when this equilibrium was disturbed, forgetting would occur.

Not surprisingly, the first person to introduce a really major idea in the field of memory was Plato, in the **fourth century BC**. His theory is known as the Wax Tablet Hypothesis and was still accepted until recently. To Plato, the mind accepted impressions in the same way that wax becomes marked when a pointed object is applied to its surface. Plato assumed that once the impression had been made it remained until it wore away with time, leaving a smooth surface once again. This smooth surface was, of course, what Plato considered to be equivalent to complete forgetting – the opposite aspect of the same process. As will become clear later, many people now feel that memory and forgetting are two quite different processes. Shortly after Plato, Zeno the Stoic slightly modified Plato's ideas, suggesting that sensations actually 'wrote' impressions on the wax tablet. Like those before him, when Zeno referred to the mind and its memory, he did not place it in any particular organ or section of the body. To him, as to all the Greeks, 'mind' was a very unclear concept.

The first man to introduce a more scientific terminology was Aristotle, in the **late fourth century BC**. He maintained that the language previously used was not adequate to explain the physical aspects of memory. In applying his new language Aristotle attributed to the heart most of the functions that we now attribute to the brain. Part of the heart's function, he realised, was concerned with the blood, and he felt that memory was based on the blood's movements. He thought that forgetting was the result of a gradual slowing down of these movements. Aristotle made another important contribution to the subject of memory when he introduced his laws of association of ideas. The concept of association of ideas and images is now known to be of major importance to memory. Throughout this book this concept will be discussed and applied.

In the **third century BC**, Herophilus introduced 'vital' and 'animal' spirits to the discussion. He thought that the vital, or 'higher order', spirits produced the 'lower order' animal spirits, which included the memory, the brain and the nervous system. All of these he thought to be secondary in importance to the heart. It is interesting to note that one reason advanced by Herophilus for man's superiority over animals was the large number of creases in his brain. (These creases are now known as the convolutions of the cortex.) Herophilus, however, offered no reason for his conclusion. It was not until the nineteenth century, more than 2000 years later, that the real importance of the cortex was discovered.

The Greeks, then, were the first to seek a physical as opposed to a spiritual basis for memory; they developed scientific concepts and a language structure that helped the development of these concepts; and they contributed the Wax Tablet Hypothesis, which suggested that memory and forgetting were opposite aspects of the same process.

THE ROMANS

The theoretical contributions by the Romans to our knowledge of memory were surprisingly minimal. The major thinkers of their time, including Cicero in the **first century BC** and Quintilian in the **first**

century AD, accepted without question the Wax Tablet Hypothesis of memory and did little further work on the subject. Their major and extremely important contributions were in the development of memory systems. They were the first to introduce the idea of a Link System and a Room System, both of which will be described in later chapters.

THE INFLUENCE OF THE CHRISTIAN CHURCH

The next major contributor to memory theory was the great physician Galen in the **second century AD**. He located and delineated various anatomical and physiological structures and made further investigations into the function and structure of the nervous system. Like the later Greeks, he assumed that memory and mental processes were part of the lower order of animal spirits. He thought that these spirits were manufactured in the sides of the brain and that, consequently, memory was seated there. Galen thought that air was sucked into the brain and mixed with the vital spirits. This mixture produced animal spirits that were pushed down through the nervous system, enabling humans to experience sensation.

Galen's ideas on memory were rapidly accepted and condoned by the Church, which at this time was beginning to exert a great influence. His ideas became doctrine, and as a result little progress was made in the field for 1500 years. These intellectual strictures stifled some of the greatest minds that philosophy and science have produced. In the **fourth century AD** St Augustine accepted the Church's idea that memory was a function of the soul and that the soul was located in the brain. He never expanded on the anatomical aspects of these ideas.

From the time of St Augustine until the **seventeenth century** there were almost no significant developments, and even in the seventeenth century new ideas were restricted by doctrine. Even so great a thinker as Descartes accepted Galen's basic ideas, although he thought that animal spirits were sent from the pineal gland on special courses through the brain until they came to the part where memory could be triggered. The more clear-cut these courses, the more readily, he thought, would they open when animal spirits travelled through them. It was in this way that he explained the improvement of memory and the development of what are known as memory traces. A memory trace is a physical change in the nervous system that was not present before learning. The trace enables us to recall.

Another great philosopher, who went along with the tide, was Thomas Hobbes, who discussed and considered the idea of memory but contributed little to what had already been said. He agreed with Aristotle's ideas, rejecting nonphysical explanations of memory. He did not, however, specify the real nature of memory, nor did he make any significant attempts to locate it accurately.

It is evident from the theories of the seventeenth-century intellectuals that the inhibiting influence of Galen and the Church had been profound. Practically all these great thinkers accepted without question primitive ideas on memory.

TRANSITIONAL PERIOD – THE EIGHTEENTH CENTURY

One of the first thinkers to be influenced by the Renaissance and by the ideas of Newton was David Hartley in the **eighteenth century**, who developed the vibratory theory of memory. Applying Newton's ideas on vibrating particles, Hartley suggested that there were memory vibrations in the brain that began before birth. New sensations modified existing vibrations in degree, kind, place and direction. After being influenced by a new sensation, vibrations quickly returned to their natural state. But if the same sensation appeared again, the vibrations took a little longer to return. This progression would finally result in the vibrations remaining in their 'new' state, and a memory trace was thus established.

Other major thinkers of this period included Zanotti, who was the first to link electrical forces with brain functions, and Bonnet, who developed the ideas of Hartley in relation to the flexibility of nerve fibres. He felt that the more often nerves were used, the more easily they vibrated, and the better memory would be. The theories of these men were more sophisticated than previous ones because they had been largely influenced by developments in related scientific fields. This interaction of ideas laid the groundwork for some of the modern theories of memory.

THE NINETEENTH CENTURY

With the development of science in Germany in the **nineteenth century**, some important advances occurred. Many of the ideas initiated by the Greeks were overthrown, and work on memory expanded to include the biological sciences.

Georg Prochaska, a Czech physiologist, finally and irrevocably rejected the age-old idea of animal spirits on the grounds that it had no scientific basis and that there was no evidence to support it. He felt that limited existing knowledge made speculation on the location of memory in the brain a waste of time. 'Spatial localisation may be possible,' he said, 'but we just do not know enough at the moment to make it a useful idea.' It was not for some 50 years that localising the area of memory function became a useful pursuit.

Another major theory presented in this century was that of Pierre Flourens, a French physiologist, who 'located' the memory in every part of the brain. He said that the brain acted as a whole and could not be considered as the interaction of elementary parts.

MODERN THEORIES

Developments in memory research have been aided to an enormous degree by advances in technology and methodology in the **twentieth century**. Almost without exception physiologists and other thinkers in this field agree that memory is located in the cerebrum, which is the large area of the brain covering the surface of the cortex. Even today, however, the exact localisation of memory areas is proving a difficult task, as is the accurate understanding of the function of memory itself. Current thought has progressed from Hermann Ebbinghaus's work, at the turn of the century, with regard to basic learning and forgetting curves (see chapter 11), to advanced and complex theories. Research and theory can be roughly divided into three main areas: work on establishing a biochemical basis for memory; theories suggesting that memory can no longer be considered as a single process but must be broken down into divisions; and the clinical surgeon Wilder Penfield's work on brain stimulation.

Research into the biochemical basis for memory was initiated in the *late 1950s*. This theory suggests that RNA (ribonucleic acid), a complex molecule, serves as a chemical mediator for memory. RNA is produced by the substance DNA (deoxyribonucleic acid), which is responsible for our genetic inheritance. For example, DNA determines eye colour. A number of experiments have been performed with RNA that lend support to the idea that RNA does indeed have a lot to do with the way in which we remember things. In one instance, when animals were given certain types of training, the RNA found in specific cells was changed. And further, if the production of RNA in an animal's body was stopped or modified, this animal was unable to learn or remember. An even more exciting experiment showed that when RNA was taken from one rat and injected into another, the second rat 'remembered' things that he had never been taught but that the first rat had.

While research into this aspect of memory is progressing, other theorists are saying that we should stop emphasising 'memory' and concentrate more on the study of 'forgetting'. Their position is that we do not so much remember as gradually forget. Encompassing this idea is the duplex theory of remembering and forgetting, which states that there are two different kinds of information retention: long-term and short-term. For example, you have probably experienced a different 'feeling' in the way that you recall a telephone number that has just been given to you and the way that you recall your own telephone number. The short-term situation is one in which the idea is 'in' the brain but has not yet been properly coded and is therefore more readily forgotten. In the long-term situation the idea has been completely coded, filed and stored, and it will probably remain there for years, if not for life.

Research into direct brain stimulation was initiated by Dr Wilder Penfield. When performing craniotomies (removal of a small section of the brain) in order to reduce epileptic attacks, Penfield had first to remove a portion of the skull lying over the side of the brain. Before operating, Penfield conducted a systematic electrical stimulation of the open brain, and the patient, who remained conscious, reported his experience after each stimulation. In an early case Penfield stimulated the temporal lobe of the brain, and the patient reported a re-created memory of a childhood experience.

Penfield found that stimulating various areas of the cortex produces a range of responses but that only stimulation of the temporal lobes leads to reports of meaningful and integrated experiences. These experiences are often complete in that when re-created they include the colour, sound, movement and emotional content of the original experiences.

Of particular interest in these studies is the fact that some of the memories stimulated electrically by Penfield had been unavailable in normal recall. In addition, the stimulated experiences seemed to be far more specific and accurate than normal conscious recall, which tends to be a generalisation. It was Penfield's belief that the brain records every item to which it pays conscious attention and that this record is basically permanent, although it may be 'forgotten' in day-to-day living.

More recently, theorists have returned to a position similar to that of Flourens, in which they are suggesting that every part of the brain may include *all* memories. This model is based on holographic photography. In simple terms, a holographic photographic plate is simply a piece of glass, which, when two laser beams are passed through it at the right angle, reproduces a ghostly, three-dimensional photograph. One of the amazing things about this photographic plate is that if you smash it into 100 pieces and take any one of those 100 pieces, you can shine the two laser beams through it and still get the same (although slightly more blurred) picture. Thus every part of the holographic photographic plate contains a minirecord of the overall picture.

British scientist David Bohm and others are suggesting that the brain is similar. In other words, every one of our multimillion brain cells may, in fact, act as a minibrain, recording in some fantastically complex way, as yet indiscernible to our clumsy measuring instruments, our entire experience. Fantastic as this theory may sound, it goes a long way toward explaining the perfect memories we have in dreams, the surprise random recall, the memories of the perfect memorisers, the statistics from Rosensweig's experiments, the results of Penfield's experiments, the mathematical grandeur of Anokhin's results, and much of the near-death-type experiences.

Even now we are still on the threshold of a wondrous new world of knowledge, similar to that of the first people who began to explore our planet immediately after having discovered that they could make boats.

HOW MANY BRAINS?

Supplementing this modern research has been the new discovery that we have not one brain but many. Professor Roger Sperry recently received the Nobel Prize for his breakthrough work in this area. Sperry discovered that each one of us has a brain that is divided into two upper physiological sections, each dealing with different mental functions.

In the 1980s Sperry's work has been continued by Professor Eran Zaidel, who has shown that the range of cortical skills is much more widely distributed than had originally been thought. Zaidel has demonstrated that *both* cerebral hemispheres seem to have a latent ability to perform the full range of cortical skills.

These skills, which we now know are attributable to the *entire* cortex, were originally thought to be divided into the left and right hemispheres in the following way:

The left side of the cortex processes in the following manner:

1 logic
2 words
3 lists
4 number
5 sequence
6 linearity
7 analysis

Similarly, in most of us, the right side of the cortex processes with the following mental functions:

1 rhythm
2 imagination
3 daydreaming
4 colour
5 dimension
6 spacial awareness
7 *Gestalt* (whole picture)

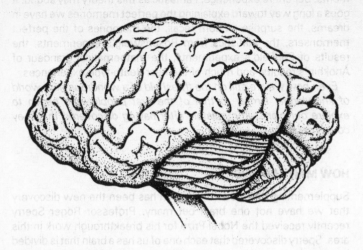

This is your superstreamlined brain, depicted as if viewed with X-ray eyes from a vantage point to the left of the left shoulder. Thus, you are looking at the left cortex, which deals with the mental functions of logic, words, lists, number, sequence, linearity, and analysis. The right side of the cortex, the back tip of which you can just see, deals with rhythm, imagination, daydreaming, colour, dimension, spacial awareness and *Gestalt*. These two ranges of abilities *combine* to give you a super-powered memory.

No matter what you have been taught, somewhere latent within each of you lies each one of these capabilities simply waiting to be freed. Sperry and others also found that the more people use both sides of their brains together, the more the use of each side benefits the other. For example, it was found that the study of music helped the study of mathematics, and the study of mathematics helped the study of music; that the study of rhythm helped the study of languages and that the study of languages helped the learning of bodily rhythms; that the study of dimension helped the study of mathematics and that the study of mathematics helped the brain conceptualise dimension; and so on. It was similarly found that if a person used more of these areas, the more generally capable was his entire memory.

4 | The secret principles underlying a superpower memory

The Greeks so worshipped memory that they made a goddess out of her – Mnemosyne. It was her name from which was derived the current word *mnemonics*, used to describe memory techniques such as those you are about to learn. In Greek and Roman times, senators would learn these techniques in order to impress other politicians and the public with their phenomenal powers of learning and memory. Using these simple but sophisticated methods, the Romans were able to remember, without fault, thousands of items, including statistics relating to their empire, and became the rulers of their time.

Long before we had discovered the physiological breakdown of the functions in the left and right cortical structures, the Greeks had intuitively realised that there are two underlying principles that ensure perfect memory:

imagination
association

Whereas, in current times, most of us are actively discouraged from using our imaginative abilities, and consequently learn very little about the nature of mental association, the Greeks emphasised these two foundation stones of mental functioning and opened the way for us to develop the techniques even further.

Quite simply, if you want to remember *anything*, all you have to do is to *associate* (link) it with *some known or fixed item* (the memory systems in this book will give you those easily remembered fixed items), calling upon your *imagination* throughout.

THE MEMORY PRINCIPLES

The principles for perfect memory laid down by the Greeks fit in *exactly* with the information recently discovered about the left and right cortex. Without a scientific basis, the Greeks realised that in order to remember well, you have to use every aspect of your mind. In the following pages of this chapter these principles will be outlined.

In order to remember well, you must include in your associated and linked mental landscape the following:

1 Synaesthesia/Sensuality
Synaesthesia refers to the blending of the senses. Most of the great 'natural' memorisers and all of the great mnemonists developed an increased sensitivity in each of their senses, and then blended these senses to produce enhanced recall. In developing the memory it was found to be essential to sensitise increasingly and train regularly your:

a) vision
b) hearing
c) sense of smell
d) taste
e) touch
f) kinaesthesia – your awareness of bodily position and movement in space.

2 Movement
In any mnemonic image, movement adds another giant range of possibilities for your brain to 'link in' and thus remember. As your images move, make them three dimensional. As a subdivision of movement, use rhythm in your memory images. The more rhythm and variation of rhythm in your mental picture, the more they will be outstanding and thus the more they will be remembered.

3 Association
Whatever you wish to memorise, make sure you associate or link it to something stable in your mental environment, i.e. Peg system: one = paintbrush. (See page 51.)

4 Sexuality
We all have a good memory in this area. Use it!

5 Humour
The more funny, ridiculous, absurd and surreal you make your images, the more outstandingly memorable they will be. Have fun with your memory.

6 Imagination
This is the powerhouse of your memory. Einstein said, 'Imagination is more important than knowledge. For knowledge is limited,

whereas imagination embraces the entire world, stimulating progress, giving birth to evolution.' The more you apply your vivid imagination to memory, the better your memory will be. (Memory Foundation)

7 Number
Numbering adds specificity and efficiency to the principle of order and sequence.

8 Symbolism
Substituting a more meaningful image for a normal, boring or abstract concept increases the probability of recall, or using traditional symbols i.e. stop sign or light bulb.

9 Colour
Where appropriate, and whenever possible, use the full range of the rainbow, to make your ideas more 'colourful' and therefore more memorable.

10 Order and/or Sequence
In combination with the other principles, order and/or sequence allows for much more immediate reference, and increases the brain's possibilities for 'random access'. Examples are: little to big, colour grouping, sorting by category.

11 Positive Images
In most instances positive and pleasant images were found to be better for memory purposes, because they made the brain *want* to return to the images. Certain negative images, even though applying all the principles above, and though in and of themselves 'memorable' could be blocked by the brain because it found the prospect of returning to such images unpleasant.

12 Exaggeration
In all your images, exaggerate size, shape and sound and therefore memorability.

The basic Memory Principles can themselves be memorised by using an anagram. They have been ordered on the preceding pages to make the phrase SMASHIN' SCOPE, which confirms the 'smashin' scope' of your limitless memory.

KEY MEMORY IMAGE WORDS

In each memory system there is a Key Word. This word is the 'Key Memory Word' in that it is the constant peg on which you will hang other items you wish to remember. This Key Memory Word is specifically designed to be an 'Image Word' in that it *must* produce a picture or image in the mind of the person using the memory system. Thus the phrase 'Key Memory Image Word'.

Purity
As you progress through the increasingly sophisticated mnemonic systems outlined in the following chapters, you will realise the importance of being sure that the pictures you build in your mind contain only the items you want to remember, and those items must be associated with or connected to Key Memory Images. The connections between your basic Memory System Images and the things you wish to remember should be as fundamental, pure and uncomplicated as possible.

This may be accomplished as follows:

1 Crashing things together
2 Sticking things together
3 Placing things on top of each other
4 Placing things underneath each other
5 Placing things inside each other
6 Substituting things for each other
7 Placing things in new situations
8 Weaving things together
9 Wrapping things together
10 Having things talk
11 Having things dance
12 Having things share their colour, aroma, action

By now it will be clear to you that the systems worked out by the Greeks, and for nearly 2000 years discarded as mere tricks, were in fact based on the way in which the human brain actually functions. The ancients realised the importance of words, order, sequence and number, now known to be functions of the left side of the cortex; and imagination, colour, rhythm, dimension and daydreaming, now known to be right-cortex functions.

Mnemosyne was to the Greeks the most beautiful of all the goddesses, proved by the fact that Zeus spent more time in her bed than in that of any other goddess or mortal. He slept with her for nine days and nights, and the result of that coupling was the birth of the nine Muses, the goddesses who preside over love poetry, epic poetry, hymns, dance, comedy, tragedy, music, history and astronomy. For the Greeks, then, the infusion of energy (Zeus) into memory (Mnemosyne) produced both creativity and knowledge.

They were correct. If you apply the Mnemonic Principles and Techniques appropriately, not only will your memory improve in the various areas outlined in this book but your creativity will soar, and with the twin improvements in memory and creativity, your overall mental functioning and assimilation of knowledge will accelerate at the same fantastic pace. In the process you will be developing a new and dynamic synthesis between the left and right cortex of your brain.

The following chapters take you step by step through first the very simple systems and then the more advanced systems, concluding with the Major System, the Star of the Memorisers' Solar System, which will enable you to remember as many *thousands* of items as you wish. In order that you can maintain the extraordinary results that you are going to achieve, a final chapter shows you how to adjust and maintain your memory over a long period of future time.

poetry, hymns, dance, comedy, tragedy, music, history and astronomy. For the Greeks, then, the infusion of energy (Zeus) into memory (Mnemosyne) produced both creativity and knowledge.

They were correct. If you apply the Mnemonic Principles and Techniques appropriately, not only will your memory improve on the various areas outlined in this book but your creativity will soar, and with the twin improvements in memory and creativity your overall mental functioning and assimilation of knowledge will accelerate at the same fantastic pace. In the process you will be developing a new and dynamic synthesis between the left and right cortex of your brain.

The following chapters take you step by step through first the very simple systems and then the more advanced systems, concluding with the Major System, the Star of the Mnemonics' Solar System, which will enable you to remember as many thousands of items as you wish. In order that you can maintain the extraordinary results that you are going to achieve, a final chapter shows you how to adjust and maintain your memory over a long period of future time.

5 The Link System

In this chapter you will see for yourself that your memory can improve, and that by improving it, your imaginative powers and your creativity will also be released. The Link System is the most basic of all the memory systems and will give you a foundation with which to make learning the most advanced systems extremely easy. This basic system is used for memorising short lists of items, such as shopping lists, in which each item is linked to or associated with the next. While using this system, you will be using all of these Memory Principles:

sensuality
movement
association
sexuality
humour
imagination
number
symbolism
colour
order and/or sequence
positive images
exaggeration

You will also be using:

contraction
absurdity
rhythm
taste
touch
smell
sight
hearing
substitution

In using these Principles you will be exercising the dynamic relationship between your left and right cortex and thereby increasing the overall power of your brain. Imagine, for example, that you have been asked to shop for the following items:

a silver serving spoon
six drinking glasses
bananas
pure soap
eggs
biological washing powder
dental floss
wholewheat bread
tomatoes
roses

Instead of scrambling around for little bits of paper (everyone has either done it himself or seen others desperately fumbling through their pockets for the missing slip) or trying to remember all the items by simple repetition and consequently forgetting at least two or three, you would simply apply the Memory Principles in the following way.

Imagine yourself walking out of your front door perfecting the most amazing balancing trick: in your mouth is the most enormous silver-coloured serving spoon, the handle-end of which you are holding between your teeth, as you *taste* and *feel* the metal in your mouth.

Carefully balanced in the ladle-end of the spoon are six *exaggeratedly* beautiful crystal glasses, through which the sunlight reflects brilliantly into your bedazzled eyes. As you look with delighted amazement at the glasses, you can also *hear* them deliberately tinkling on the silver spoon. Going outside into the street, you step on the most *gigantic yellow and brown coloured* banana, which *skids* with a *swish* from under you. Being a fantastic balancer, you barely manage not to fall and confidently place your other foot groundward only to find that you have stepped on a shimmering white bar of pure soap. This being too much for even a master, you fall backward and land seat down on a mound of eggs. As you sink into them, you can *hear* the cracking of the shells, *see* the yellow of the yolk and the white of the albumen, and *feel* the dampness soaking into your clothes. (See Colour Plate I.)

Using your *imaginative* ability to *exaggerate* anything, you speed up time and *imagine* that, in a couple of seconds, you have gone back inside, undressed, washed your soiled clothes in a super biological washing powder, called pure soap, which allows pure, shimmering water to leave the washing machine, and then visualise yourself once again on your way out of the front door. This time, because you are slightly tired by the previous accident, you are pulling yourself along towards the shops on a *gigantic* rope made of *millions* of threads of dental floss, the rope *connecting* your front door to the chemist's shop.

Just as all this exertion begins to make you feel hungry, wafting on the warm wind comes an *incredibly strong aroma* of freshly baked wholewheat bread. *Imagine* yourself being dragged by the nose as you salivate *extraordinarily* thinking of the *taste* of the freshly baked bread. As you enter the baker's shop, you notice to your amazement that every loaf on the baker's shelves is filled with *brilliantly pulsating red* tomatoes, the baker's latest idea for a new food fad.

As you walk out of the baker's shop, *noisily* munching on your tomato and wholewheat loaf, you see walking down the road with the most amazing *rhythm* the *sexiest* person you have ever seen (really let your imagination go on this one). Your immediate instinct is to buy the person roses, so you dive into the nearest flower shop, which sells nothing but red roses, and buy the lot, *bedazzled* by the *greenness* of the leaves, the *redness* of the flowers, the *feel* of the flowers as you carry them, the *feel* of the thorns, and the *fragrance* from the roses themselves.

When you have finished reading this fantasy, close your eyes and run back through the image-story you have just completed. If you think you can already remember all ten items in the shopping list, turn now to the next page and fill in the answers. If not, read through this chapter again, carefully visualising on your mind's inner screen, in sequence, the events of the story. Turn to the next page when you are ready.

MEMORY TEST

Note here the ten items you had to buy.

_____

_____

_____

_____

_____

_____

_____

_____

_____

_____

If you scored 7 or more, you are already in the top 1 per cent of scores for the memorisation of such a list. And you have now used the basic keys for unlocking much of the limitless potential of your brain.

Practise the Link System on a couple of lists of your own devising, making sure that you use the Memory Principles throughout, remembering that the more imaginative, absurd and sensual you can be, the better. When you have had a little practice with the Link System, move on to the next chapter.

6 The Number-Shape System

In chapter 5 you learned the Link System, in which you applied all the Memory Principles with the exception of number and order. We now move on to the first of the Peg Memory Systems. A Peg Memory System differs from the Link System in that it uses a special list of Key Memory Images that never change and to which everything that you wish to remember can be linked and associated. A Peg System can be thought of much like a wardrobe containing a certain definite number of hangers on which you hang your clothes. The hangers themselves never change, but the clothes that are hung on them vary infinitely. In the Number-Shape System, which is the first of the Peg Systems covered, the number and shape represent the hangers, and the things you wish to remember with the system represent the clothes to be hung on the hangers. The system is an easy one and uses only the numbers from 1 to 10.

The best system is one you will create yourself – rather than one supplied for you. This is because minds are infinitely varied, and the associations, links and images that you may have will generally be different from mine and everyone else's. The associations and images you generate from your own creative imagination will last far longer and be much more effective than any that could be 'implanted'. I shall therefore explain exactly how you can construct a system and shall then give examples of its practical use.

In the Number-Shape System, all you have to do is think of images for each of the numbers from 1 to 10, each image reminding you of the number because both the image and the number have the same shape. For example, and to make your task a little easier, the Key Number-Shape Memory Word that most people use for the number 2 is *swan* because the number 2 is shaped like a swan, and similarly because a swan looks like a living, elegant version of the number 2.

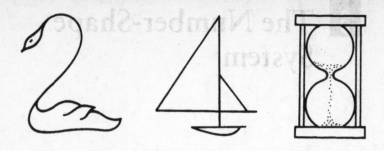

In the Number-Shape System, images that 'look like' the number are used as hangers, or hooks, on which to link items you wish to remember. For example, a common Key Image for the number 2 is a swan.

Listed opposite are the numbers from 1 to 10, with a blank beside each number for you to pencil in the various words that you think *best* image the shape of the numbers. As you select the words, try to make sure that they are exceptionally good *visual* images, with lots of good colour and basic imagination-potential within them. They should be images to which you will be able to link the things you wish to remember with ease and enjoyment.

Here are several examples:
1 **Paintbrush**, pole, pencil, pen, penis, straw, candle
2 **Swan**, duck, goose
3 **Heart**, breasts, double chin, behind, molehills
4 **Yacht**, table, chair
5 **Hook**, cymbal and drum, pregnant woman
6 **Elephant's trunk**, golf club, cherry, pipe
7 **Cliff**, fishing line, boomerang
8 **Snowman**, bun, hourglass, shapely woman
9 **Balloon and stick**, tennis racquet, sperm, tadpole, flag
10 **Bat and ball**, Laurel and Hardy

Give yourself not more than ten minutes to complete the list from 1 to 10, and even if you find some numbers difficult, don't worry; just read on.

1 _____

2 _____

3 _____

4 _____

5 _____

6 _____

7 _____

8 _____

9 _____

10 _____

Now that you have generated several of your own number-images and have seen other suggestions, you should select the Number-Shape Key Memory *Image* for each number that is the best one for you.

When you have done this, draw in overleaf your appropriate image for each number. (Don't feel inhibited if you consider yourself not good at art; your right brain needs the practice.) The more colours you can use in your images, the better.

At the end of this paragraph you should close your eyes and test yourself by mentally running through the numbers from 1 to 10 in order. As you come to each number, mentally link it with the Number-Shape Key Memory Image you have selected and drawn, using the Memory Principles throughout, especially exaggeration, colour and movement. Make sure you actually *see* the images on the videoscreen of your closed eyelids, or hear, experience, taste or smell them. When you have done this exercise once, run through the numbers in reverse order, again linking them with your chosen word and again applying the Memory Principles. Next, pick out numbers randomly and as quickly as you can, making a game to see how quickly the image comes to mind. And finally reverse the whole process by flashing the images on your internal videoscreen, seeing how quickly you can connect the basic numbers to your images. Do this exercise now.

Number	Number-Shape Key Memory Image
1	
2	
3	
4	
5	
6	
7	
8	
9	
10	

You have already accomplished a memory feat that most people would find difficult. You have now forged into your memory and creative imagination a system that you will be able to use throughout your life and that combines the qualities of both the left and right of your brain.

The use of the system is simple and enjoyable and involves the other major memory device: **linking/association**. For example, if you have a list of ten items that you wish to remember not simply by linking, as in the previous chapter, but in numerical order, reverse numerical order and random numerical order, the Number-Shape System makes the whole process easy. Let us put it to the test:

Assume you wish to remember the following list of items:

1	Symphony	6	Sunshine
2	Prayer	7	Apple pie
3	Watermelon	8	Blossoms
4	Volcano	9	Spaceship
5	Motorcycle	10	Field of wheat

To remember these items in *any* order, all that you have to do is to link them with the appropriate Number-Shape Key Memory Image. As with the Link System, and all memory systems, the Memory Principles should be applied throughout; the more imaginative you can be, the better. Give yourself not more than three minutes to complete your memorisation of these ten items, using the Number-Shape System, and then fill in the answers below. Fill in both your Number-Shape Image Words and the items you were asked to remember with each number. If you feel confident, start this exercise now; if not, you may find it helpful to read the examples given on pages 56–7 before testing yourself.

1 _____ _____

2 _____ _____

3 _____ _____

4 _____ _____

5 _____ _____

6 _____ _____

7 _____ _____

8 _____ _____

9 _____ _____

10 _____ _____

As a guide for those who might have had a little difficulty with this exercise, the following are examples of possible ways in which the ten items to be memorised might have been linked to the Number-Shape Key Memory Images:

1 For **symphony** you might have imagined a conductor conducting frantically with a gigantic **paintbrush,** splattering paint over most of the musicians; or you might have imagined all the violinists playing their instruments with straws; or again you might have imagined them all with gigantic penises. Whatever your image, the Memory Principles should be applied.

2 Prayer is an abstract word. It is often mistakenly assumed that abstract words are hard to memorise. Using proper memory techniques, you will find that this is not the case, as you may have already discovered. All you have to do is to 'image' the abstract in concrete form. You might have to imagine your **swan** or duck or goose with its wings upheld like hands in prayer; or filled an imaginary church with imaginary swans, geese or ducks being led in a prayer service by a minister who was also a bird.

3 Easy!

4 You might have imagined your gigantic **volcano** within the ocean, seeing it erupting red and furiously beneath your **yacht**, the steam and hissing created by the volcano actually heaving your yacht right off the water; or you might have had your volcano miniaturised and placed on a chair on which you were about to sit (you would certainly *feel* it); or imagined a mountainous table actually blocking the power of the volcano.

5 A giant **hook** might have come down from the sky and lifted you and your **motorcycle** off the road along which you were speeding; or you on your motorcycle might have crashed, incredibly noisily and disruptively, into a musical instrument shop, knocking over cymbals and drums; or seated astride the motorcycle is an enormous pregnant woman.

6 Sunshine could be pouring out of an **elephant's trunk**; or you might have flung the golf club rhythmically up into the air, and it got entangled in a sunbeam and drawn toward the sun; or the sunbeam could be zapping like a laser into a cherry, making it grow gigantic before your very eyes, and you imagine the taste as you bite into it, the juices dribbling down your chin.

7 Your gigantic **cliff** could actually be made entirely of **apple pie**; or your fishing line could catch, instead of a fish, a bedraggled, soggy but nevertheless still scrumptious apple pie; or your boomerang could fly off into the distance and, with a thunk, end up in an apple pie as big as a mountain, not returning to you but sending only the delicious smells of the apple and the piecrust.

8 Your **snowman** could be decorated entirely with exquisitely pink **blossoms**; or your hourglass could tell the time not by the falling of sand but by the gentle falling of millions of tiny blossoms within the hourglass; or your shapely woman could be walking provocatively through endless fields of waist-high fallen blossoms.

9 You could miniaturise your **spaceship** and make it into a **balloon and stick;** or miniaturise it even further and have it as the leading sperm about to fertilise an egg; or imagine it leaving Earth's atmosphere with a huge flag on its nose.

10 You feel the shock in your **bat** as it cracks against the **ball,** and you see the ball sailing across endless **fields** of rhythmically waving, beautifully golden **wheat**; or you image Laurel and Hardy playing the ultimate fools and thrashing around, while tramping, the same endless fields of wheat.

These are, of course, only examples, and are included to indicate the kind of exaggeration, imagination, sensuality and creative thinking that is necessary to establish the most effective memory links. As with the Link System, it is essential that you practise this system on your own. I recommend giving yourself at least one test before you move to the next chapter.

One of the best ways to do this is to check yourself with members of your family or with friends. Ask them to make up a list of any 10 items and to read the list to you with about a five- to ten-second pause between each item. The instant they have given you the item to be memorised, make the most wild, colourful, exaggerated associations possible, projecting images onto your internal screen, and thus consolidating them as you progress. You (and they) will be amazed at the ease with which you can remember the items, and it is most impressive when you are able to repeat them in reverse and random order.

Don't worry about confusing previous lists of items with new ones. As mentioned at the beginning of the chapter, this particular Peg System can be compared to coat hangers – you simply remove one coat (association) and replace it with another.

In the next chapter I shall introduce a second system based on the numbers 1 to 10: the Number-Rhyme System. These two systems can then be combined to enable you to remember 20 items with as much facility as you have just remembered 10. In subsequent chapters more sophisticated systems will be introduced to allow you to store lists of items stretching into the thousands. These systems are recommended for long-term memory, the things you wish to retain over a long period of time. The Number-Shape System you have just learned and the Number-Rhyme System you are about to learn are recommended for your short-term memory purposes – those items you wish to remember for only a few hours.

Give yourself about a day to become skilled in using the techniques you have learned so far before moving to the next chapter.

7 The Number-Rhyme System

You will find the Number-Rhyme System especially easy to learn, since it is identical in principle to the Number-Shape System. Also, like the Number-Shape System, it can be used for remembering short lists of items that you need to store in your memory for only a brief time. In this system, as before, you use the numbers from 1 to 10, and instead of having Key Memory Images that resemble the shape of the number, you devise Key Memory Images represented by a word that *rhymes* with the sound of the number. For example, the Key Rhyming Memory Image Word that most people use for the number 5 is *hive*, the images that they use ranging from one enormous hive from which emanates a sky-covering swarm of monster bees to a microscopic hive with only one tiny bee.

As with the Link System and the Number-Shape System, it is essential to apply the Memory Principles, making each image as imaginative, colourful and sensual as you possibly can. As in the previous chapter, you will find listed the numbers from 1 to 10, with a blank beside each for you to pencil in the Rhyming Image Word that you think will produce the best image for each number. Make sure that the images will be good memory hooks for you. You may select them from the list on page 60.

By now your associative and creative thinking abilities will have improved your mental capacity, so give yourself not ten minutes as before but six minutes to fill in your initial Key Image Words.

Number	Number-Rhyme Image Word
1	
2	
3	
4	

5
6
7
8
9
10

As before, I am going to offer a few alternative image ideas commonly used. Consider these and your own Key Rhyming Image Words, and select for each number, from 1 to 10, the one you consider to be best for you:

1	**Bun**, sun, nun, Hun	**1**	run
2	**Shoe**, pew, loo, crew, gnu	**2**	coo
3	**Tree**, flea, sea, knee	**3**	see
4	**Door**, moor, boar, paw	**4**	pour
5	**Hive**, jive, drive, chive	**5**	dive
6	**Sticks**, bricks, wicks, licks	**6**	kicks
7	**Heaven**, Devon	**7**	leaven
8	**Skate**, bait, gate, date	**8**	ate
9	**Vine**, wine, twine, line	**9**	dine
10	**Hen**, pen, den, wren, men	**10**	yen

Having chosen the most appropriate Key Rhyming Image Word, draw your image, using as much imagination and colour as possible, in the space provided below.

Number	Number-Rhyme Key Image
1	
2	
3	

After you have finished reading this paragraph, test yourself with your chosen Key Rhyming Image. Close your eyes, and run through the numbers 1 to 10, projecting onto your inner screen a clear and brilliant picture of the Key Rhyming Image you have for each number. First, run through the system from 1 to 10 in the normal order; next, run through the system in reverse order; next, run through the system in random order; finally, pick the images 'out of the air', and connect the numbers to them. As you do each exercise,

repeat it, making each repetition faster than the previous one, until you acquire such skill that your mind will instantaneously produce the image as soon as you think of the number. Spend at least five minutes on this exercise, starting now.

Now that you have mastered the Number-Rhyme System, you will see that it can be used in exactly the same way as the Number-Shape System.

Having learned both these systems, you have not only two separate 1 to 10 systems but also the makings of a system that allows you to remember *twenty* objects in standard sequence, reverse sequence and random sequence. All you have to do is to establish one of these two systems as the numbers from 1 to 10, letting the other system represent the numbers from 11 to 20. Decide which system you want to be which, and immediately put it to the test!

Give yourself approximately five minutes to memorise the list given below. When your time is up, fill in the answers as explained in the paragraph below.

1	Atom	11	Glitter
2	Tree	12	Heater
3	Stethoscope	13	Railway
4	Sofa	14	Lighter
5	Alley	15	Wart
6	Tile	16	Star
7	Windscreen	17	Peace
8	Honey	18	Button
9	Brush	19	Pram
10	Toothpaste	20	Pump

NUMBER-SHAPE AND NUMBER-RHYME MEMORY TEST

Opposite are three columns of 20 numbers: the first in standard order; the second in reverse order; the third in random order. Complete each list, filling in, next to the number, the appropriate item from the list you have just memorised, covering the lists with your hand or with paper as you complete them and start on the next. When you have finished, calculate your score out of a possible 60 points.

1	20	11
2	19	15
3	18	10
4	17	3
5	16	17
6	15	20
7	14	4
8	13	9
9	12	5
10	11	19
11	10	8
12	9	13
13	8	1
14	7	18
15	6	7
16	5	16
17	4	6
18	3	12
19	2	2
20	1	14

Score, out of 60 points: _____

If it initially doesn't work perfectly . . .

You will almost certainly have made an improvement over your performance in the original test, but you might find that you are still having difficulty with certain associations. Check any such 'weak' associations and examine the reasons for any failure. These reasons usually include: associations that you don't like; too close or too similar associations; not enough exaggeration and imagination; not enough colour; not enough movement; weak links; not enough sensuality; and not enough humour. Take confidence from the fact that the more you practise, the more such weak links will become a matter of history. Today and tomorrow test yourself whenever pos-

sible. Ask as many of your friends and acquaintances as possible to try and catch you out on lists that they make up for you to remember.

On the first few attempts, you will undoubtedly make some errors, but even so you will be performing far beyond the average. Consider any errors and mistakes you make to be good opportunities for examining – and subsequently strengthening – any areas of weakness in your memory systems and the way you apply them. If you persevere, you will soon be able to fire back lists given to you without any hesitation and without any fear of failure. You will then be able to use the systems confidently – for pleasure, for entertainment, for practical use, and for exercising your general memory.

As you become more skilled, keep a continuing and growing list of the areas in your life in which you will apply the systems you are currently learning.

In the next chapter you will learn the basic system used and developed by the first recorded masters of mnemonics, the Romans.

The Roman Room System

The Romans were great inventors and practitioners of mnemonic techniques, one of their most popular being the Roman Room. The Romans constructed such a system easily. They imagined the entrance to their house and their room and then filled the room with as many objects and items of furniture as they chose – each object and piece of furniture serving as a link-image onto which they attached the things they wished to remember. The Romans were particularly careful not to make a mental rubbish dump of their room; precision and order (attributes of the left side of your cortex) are essential in this system.

A Roman might, for example, have constructed his imaginary entrance and room with two gigantic pillars at either side of the front door, a carved lion's head as his doorknob, and an exquisite Greek statue on the immediate left as he walked in. Next to the statue might have been a large sofa covered with the fur of one of the animals the Roman had hunted; next to the sofa a flowering plant; and, in front of the sofa, a large marble table on which were placed goblets, a wine container, a bowl of fruit, and so forth.

Let's say that the Roman then wished to remember to buy a pair of sandals, to get his sword sharpened, to buy a new servant, to tend to his grapevine, to polish his helmet, to buy a present for his child, and so on. He would simply imagine the first pillar at the entrance of his imaginary room festooned with thousands of sandals, the leather polished and glistening, and the smell delighting his nostrils; he would imagine sharpening his sword on the right-hand pillar, hearing the scraping as he did so, and feeling the blade as it became sharper and sharper; his servant he would imagine riding a roaring lion, while grapes he might remember by imagining his exquisite statue totally entwined with a grapevine on which were luscious grapes that he could imagine seeing and tasting so well that he would actually salivate; his helmet he could imagine by substituting the container of his imaginary flowering plant with the helmet itself; finally, he could imagine himself on his sofa, his arm around the child for whom he wished to buy a gift. (See Colour Plate II.)

The Roman Room System is particularly amenable to the use of the left and right cortex, and to the Memory Principles, because it requires very precise structuring and ordering, as well as a lot of imagination and sensuality. The delight of this system is that the room is *entirely* imaginary, so you can have in it every wonderful item that you wish: things that please all your senses, items of furniture and objects of art you have always desired to possess in real life, and similarly foods and decorations that especially appeal to you. Another major advantage of using this system is that if you begin to imagine yourself in possession of certain items that exist in your imaginary room, both your memory and creative intelligence will begin to work subconsciously on ways in which you can actually acquire such objects, increasing the probability that you will eventually do so.

The Roman Room System eliminates all boundaries on your imagination and allows you to remember as many items as you wish. On page 67 there is space for you to jot down quickly your first thoughts on the items you would like to have in your room, the shape and design of your room, and so on. When you have completed this, draw your ideal Memory Room on page 68, either as an artist's drawing or as an architect's plan, both drawing and printing in the names of items with which you are going to furnish and decorate it. Many people find this to be their favourite memory system, and they use enormous sheets of paper on which they include hundreds of items in a gigantic room. If you wish to do this, by all means do so.

When you have completed this task, take a number of 'mental walks' around your room, memorising precisely the order, position and number of items in the room and similarly sensing with *all* your senses the colours, tastes, feels, smells and sounds within your room, using your whole range of cortical abilities.

As with the previous memory systems you have learned, practise memorising using the Roman Room System both alone and with friends, until the system is a firmly established technique.

ROMAN ROOM: INITIAL THOUGHTS

9 The Alphabet System

The Alphabet System is the final Peg System and is similar in construction to the Number-Shape and Number-Rhyme Systems, the only difference being that, instead of using numbers, it uses the letters of the alphabet. As with all the other memory systems, the Memory Principles apply. The rules for constructing your Alphabet Memory System are simple; they are as follows: you select a Key Memory Image Word that starts with the sound of the letter and is easily memorised. If you think of several possibilities for a letter, use the one that comes first in the dictionary. For example, for the letter L it would be possible to use *el*astic, *el*egy, *el*ephant, *el*bow, *el*m, etc. If you were looking up these words in the dictionary, the first one you would come to would be *el*astic, and that is therefore the word you would select for your Alphabet System. The reason for this rule is that if you should ever forget your Alphabet Key Image Word, you can mentally flick through the letters of the alphabet in order, rapidly arriving at the correct word. In the example given, if you had forgotten your Alphabet System image for the letter L, you would try *ela* and would immediately be able to recall your Key Image Word, *elastic*.

Another rule in the construction of your Alphabet System is that if the letter itself makes a word (for example I makes the word *eye*, and J makes the word *jay*, the bird), then that word should be used. In some cases, it is possible to use meaningful initials instead of complete words – for example, U.N.

On page 70 are listed the letters of the alphabet. Paying close attention to the now-familiar rules for constructing a system, pencil in your own initial Alphabet System Image Words after looking at the list on page 71.

Letter	Alphabet Image Word
A	
B	
C	
D	
E	
F	
G	
H	
I	
J	
K	
L	
M	
N	
O	
P	
Q	
R	
S	
T	
U	
V	
W	
X	
Y	
Z	

Now that you have completed your initial thoughts, recheck the Alphabet Image Words, making sure you have started your words with the *sound* of the letter or letter-word and not simply the letter itself. For example, *ant, bottle, case, dog* and *eddy* would not be

correct Alphabet System Image Words because they do not start
with the *sound* of the letter as it is pronounced when you are reciting
the alphabet. Having rechecked your own words, now compare
them with the following list of suggestions, and when you have
done so, select your final list.

A Ace

B Bee (the letter makes a word; this is the word that should be
used in all cases)

C Sea (the same rule applies)

D Deed (legal, though the initials DDT may be preferred)

E Easel

F Effervescence

G Jeep (or jeans)

H H-bomb

I Eye

J Jay

K Cake

L Elastic (or *elbow*, if you pronounce *elastic* with a long *e*)

M MC (emcee)

N Enamel (or *entire*, if you pronounce *enamel* with a long *e*)

O Oboe

P Pea

Q Queue

R Arch

S Eskimo

T Tea (or perhaps T-square)

U Yew

V Vehicle (or the initials V.P.)

W WC

X X-ray

Y Wife

Z Z-bend

Now make your final choices and draw your images:

FINAL ALPHABET IMAGE-WORD IMAGES

Letter	Alphabet Image-Word Image
A	
B	
C	
D	
E	
F	
G	
H	
I	

J

K

L

M

N

O

P

Q

R

S

T

U

V

W

X

Y

Z

V

W

X

Y

Z

When you have completed your Alphabet Image-Word Images, review them in exactly the same way as with the previous memory systems, mentally visualising them in standard order, reverse order and random order. Similarly, make sure you test the system individually, and then with family or friends.

Now you have learned the introductory, basic Link and Peg Memory Systems. From now on, apart from a brief summary of these concepts in the next chapter, you will be learning more advanced, expansive and sophisticated systems that will enable you to remember dates, jokes, languages, information for examinations, names and faces, books, dreams, and lists of hundreds, even thousands, of items.

10 How to increase by 100 per cent everything you have learned so far

You have now completed the five individual Memory Systems: Link, Number-Shape, Number-Rhyme, Roman Room and Alphabet Systems. Each of these systems can be used either independently or in conjunction with another system. Furthermore, one or two of the systems of your choice can be set aside, if you wish, as 'constant memory banks' if you have certain lists or orders of items that you will need to be able to recall over a period of a year or more.

Before moving on to the broader systems, however, I want to introduce you to a simple and intriguing method for instantly doubling the capacity of any of the systems you have learned to far. When you have reached the end of a system but wish to add further associations, all you have to do is to go back to the beginning of your system and imagine your association word exactly as you usually imagine it, but as if it were contained in a huge block of ice. This simple visualisation technique will drastically change the association pictures you have formed and will double the effectiveness of your system by giving you the original list plus that list in its new context.

For example, if your first key in the Number-Shape System was *paintbrush*, you would imagine that same paintbrush either buried in the heart of your giant block of ice or protruding from the corners or sides. If your first word in the Number-Rhyme System was *bun*, then you could imagine a hot bun melting the edges of the ice block in which it was contained. If your first word in the Alphabet System was *ace*, then you could imagine a giant playing card either frozen in the centre or forming one of the six sides of the ice block. If, therefore, you were using your 'second' Alphabet System (the alphabet in a huge block of ice), and the first item you wanted to remember was *parrot*, you might imagine your parrot crashing through the centre heart, spade, club or diamond of your card, shattering, with lots of squawking and cracking, the ice block.

You now have the ability to remember randomly linked items, two sets of ten items, a large number of ordered items (your Roman Room), and 26 ordered items. And you can instantly double that capacity by using the 'block of ice' method. Having reached this stage and having by now enormously increased the flexibility of your mind, your abilities to imagine, associate, sense and create are ready to take on and easily master the grandfather of all the systems: the Major System, a system that can be used to create – should you so wish – *limitless* memory systems! (See chapter 12.)

11 Your memory's rhythms

In addition to the Memory Principles you are applying throughout this book, there are two major areas that, if you understand them, will enable you to double the efficiency of your memory while you are taking in information and then to double it again after you have taken the information in: (1) recall during learning; and (2) recall after learning.

RECALL DURING A LEARNING PERIOD

In order for you to see clearly how your memory rhythms function during a standard learning period, it will be useful for you to experience a brief 'recall during a learning period' yourself. To do this, follow these instructions carefully: read the long list of words below, one word at a time, once only, *without using any memory systems or techniques, and without going back over any words*. The purpose of your reading the list will be to see how many of the words you can remember without using any of the Memory Principles. The order does not matter. So when you are reading the list, simply try to remember as many of the words as you can. Start reading now, and then test yourself on page 78.

was	the	range
away	of	of
left	beyond	and
two	Leonardo da Vinci	and
his	which	else
and	the	the
the	must	walk
far	and	room
of	of	finger
and	could	small
that	the	change

RECALL DURING LEARNING MEMORY TEST

Now that you have completed reading the list on page 77, write down below as many of the words as possible.

Now check the way in which your own memory worked: as a general principle, people remember more of what they learn at the beginning and end of a learning period, many more things that were associated with each other, and always more items that stand out in some way.

Thus, the words in this test that are commonly remembered are the first three to five words; the last two or three words; *and, of* and *the* (remembered because of repetition and linking to themselves), and *Leonardo da Vinci*, because it stands out from the rest. In addition, people will remember their own specially associated groups of words within the list, as well as words that for some personal reason are outstanding to them.

It is important to observe what was not remembered: *anything* that was not at the beginning or end of the learning period, that was not associated with other parts of the learning period, and that was not in any way outstanding. In many cases, this means that the entire bulk of the middle section of the learning period can be forgotten. Relating all of this to yourself and to time, ask yourself the following question: if you had been studying a difficult text for forty minutes, had found your understanding fairly poor throughout, and had noticed that during the last ten minutes of your reading your understanding had begun to improve slightly, would you: stop your studying immediately and conclude that as you had started to do well you could now stop and have a rest; or carry on, assuming that now your understanding was flowing more smoothly, you'd be able to keep it going until it trailed off, and *then* take your break?

Most people choose the latter of these two alternatives, assuming that if their understanding is going well all other things will also be going well. It can, however, be seen from the results of the test you have just taken, and from your own personal experience, that understanding and recall are *not* the same. They vary in amounts enormously, and the factor that defines their difference is your own time management.

What you understand you do not necessarily recall, and as time progresses while you learn, you will recall less and less of what you are understanding if you do not in some way solve the problem of the large dip in recall that occurs during the middle of the learning period (see graph page 80). This Memory Rhythm applies no matter what you are learning, and that includes the learning of memory systems. What you are looking for is a learning situation in which both recall and understanding can work in maximum harmony. You can create this situation only by organising the time in which you are learning in such a way as to enable understanding to remain high without giving the memory a chance to sag too deeply in the middle

This is easily accomplished by learning to divide your learning periods into the most beneficial time units. These units, on the average, turn out to be between 10 and 50 minutes, for example, 30 minutes, as shown in the graph on the next page. If your time is organised in this way, several advantages immediately become apparent:

1 Each of the inevitable dips in your memory during learning will not be as deep as if you had carried on without the break.

2 Instead of only two high points of recall at the beginning and end of the learning period, you will have as many as eight 'beginning and ending' high points of recall.

3 Because you are taking breaks, you will be far more rested during your next learning period than you would have been had you continued to work without breaks. The additional advantage of this is that when you are rested, both recall *and* understanding function more easily.

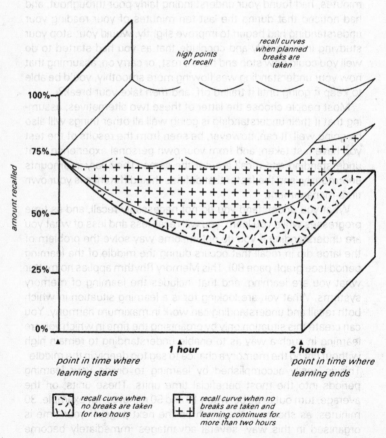

recall curves when planned breaks are taken

high points of recall

amount recalled

100%

75%

50%

25%

0%

1 hour

point in time where learning starts

2 hours

point in time where learning ends

recall curve when no breaks are taken for two hours

recall curve when no breaks are taken and learning continues for more than two hours

A graph showing which time units give maximum recall

4 Because when you are taking breaks you are both more rested and recalling more of each learning session, your comprehension of the next new section in which you find yourself after the break will be greater because you will have laid a firmer foundation in which to nourish and associate the new information. The person who has not taken such breaks, in addition to a growing fatigue, will be recalling less of what he has learned before, and therefore will be able to make continually fewer and fewer connections between the dwindling amount of information he has learned and the increasingly formidable and non-understandable information that threatens him.

5 Contrary to 'common sense', your memory of what you have learned *rises* during the breaks you take rather than immediately beginning to fall. This rise is due to the fact that your left and right hemispheres 'sort things out' for a little while on an unconscious level after you have finished taking in information during a learning period. When you return to your learning after the break you are therefore actually in possession of *more* conscious knowledge than if you had carried on without the break. This last piece of information is particularly important because it dispels those deep feelings of guilt that you may experience when you find yourself naturally taking a break but at the same time thinking that you ought to be getting 'back to the grindstone'. (See *Use Your Head* – details on page 185.)

Your breaks should usually be no longer than two to ten minutes. During each break you can allow your mind to rest by going for a short walk, making yourself a light non-alcoholic drink, doing some form of physical exercise, auto-suggesting, meditating, or listening to quiet music.

To consolidate and improve your memory even further, it is advisable at the beginning and end of each learning period to perform a very quick review and preview of what you have learned in the previous learning periods and what you are going to learn in the coming ones. This continuing review/preview cycle helps to further consolidate the information you already have, gives you growing confidence and success as you progress, allows your mind to direct itself toward the next learning target, and gives you a bird's-eye view of the territory you are going to explore mentally during your entire learning session.

Combining your knowledge of the rhythms of your memory in time during a learning period with the Memory Principles and using your creative imagination, you will be able to form imaginative links and associations throughout your period of study, consequently transforming the sags in the middle of the learning periods into nearly straight lines.

RECALL AFTER LEARNING

Once you have made it easier for your recall to work well during a learning period, it is important for you to do the same thing for your recall after the learning period. The pattern of recall after learning contains two 'surprises': first, you retain more of what you have learned *after* a few minutes have passed since the end of your learning period; second, you lose 80 per cent of the detail you have learned within 24 hours of having learned it. (You can make use of this dramatic fall to help you 'take the coats off' your 'memory coat hangers' as discussed in chapter 6.) The rise is beneficial, so you want to make use of it; the decline can be disastrous, so you usually need to make sure that it does not happen. The method for both maintaining the rise and preventing the decline is Review by Repetition.

If you have been studying for one hour, the high point in your recall after learning will occur approximately ten minutes afterwards. This high point is the ideal time for your first review. The function of your review is to imprint the information you already have in your mind, in order to make it more 'solid'. If you manage to review at the first high point, the graph of recall after learning changes, and instead of the detailed information being lost to recall, it is maintained, as shown in the graph on page 84. For example, if you had studied for one hour, your first review would take place after ten minutes and your second review would take place 24 hours later. From then on, your review should take place only when you feel the information is perhaps slipping away. On average, these reviews all occur over units of time that are based on calendar elements, i.e., days, weeks, months, years. So, you would review after one day, then after one week, then after one month, then after half a year, and so on.

Each review need take very little time. The first one should consist of a complete reviewing of your Mind Map Memory Notes (see chapter 22 and *Use Both Sides of Your Brain* — details on page 185) of information after the learning period. This may take as much as ten minutes for a one-hour learning period. After the first review, each subsequent review should consist of a quick jotting down of the basic information in your area of interest, and then a comparison of your quick notes with your basic notes. Any areas you have missed out can be filled in, and any new knowledge you may have acquired during the period between reviews can be added to your marginal notes. In this manner, your recall of all the information that you need to have constantly available can be guaranteed.

It is useful to compare the minds of people who consistently review with the minds of those who do not. People who do not review are continually putting information in and letting that same information drain out. These people will constantly find it difficult to take in new information because the background knowledge they need to understand that new information will have gone. In such a case, learning will continually be difficult, recall will always be inadequate, and the whole process of learning, understanding and recall will be unpleasant and arduous.

People who *do* review will find that with the constantly available store of increasing information, new information will slot in more easily. This will create a positive cycle in which learning, understanding and recall assist one another, making the continuing process increasingly easy. Surprisingly, the more you learn the easier it is for you to learn more. It is similar to the bibilical phrase, 'To him that hath shall be given, but from him that hath not, even that little which he hath shall be taken away.'

This information on recall after learning can also be applied to our current attitudes towards the decline of mental abilities, especially memory, with age. All our current statistics indicate that as human beings grow older their memories become increasingly worse after the age of 24. These findings, substantial as they seem, contain a major fault. They are based on surveys that studied people who generally did not have any information about how their memories worked and who consequently tended to neglect them. In other words, the tests showing that human memory declines with age were performed on people who consistently did not use the Memory Principles and did not review what they had learned. They therefore fell into the second category of the biblical statement.

Recent experiments on people who have applied the Memory Principles and who have properly managed their memory rhythms during and after learning have shown that the *opposite* of the established findings are in fact the case. If you continue to use the numerical, linguistic, analytical, logical and sequential abilities of the left side of your brain, and if you continue to use the rhythmical, musical, imaginative, colourful and dimensional abilities of the right side of your brain, along with the Memory Principles and Memory Time Rhythm – all in a continual self-educating approach – your memory will not only *not* decline with age but will actually improve enormously. The more it is fed, the more it will enable you to build up **imaginative** and **associative** networks with new areas of knowledge, and thus the more it will be able to both remember and create.

The more you give to your memory, then, the more your memory will give back to you, and with compound interest.

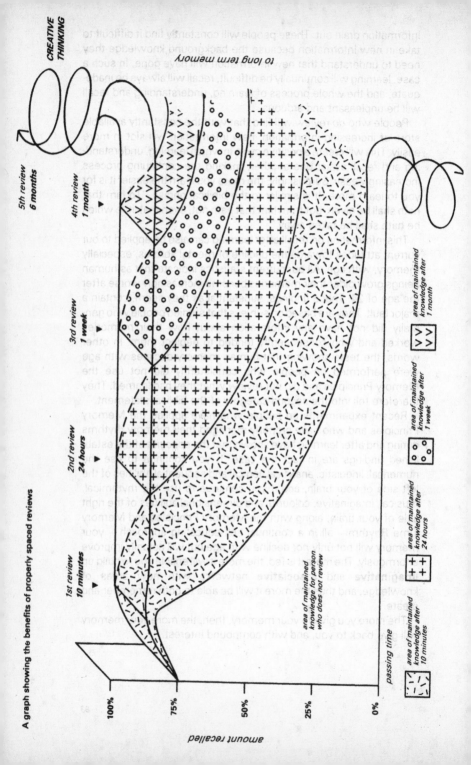

A graph showing the benefits of properly spaced reviews

CREATIVE THINKING

to long term memory

5th review
6 months

4th review
1 month

3rd review
1 week

2nd review
24 hours

1st review
10 minutes

passing time

amount recalled

100%

75%

50%

25%

0%

area of maintained knowledge after 1 month

area of maintained knowledge after 1 week

area of maintained knowledge after 24 hours

area of maintained knowledge after 10 minutes

area of maintained knowledge for person who does not review

PART II: MEMORY – THE MAJOR SYSTEM

12 The Major System

The Major System is the ultimate Basic Memory System. It has been used and continually improved upon for more than 300 years, since the middle of the seventeenth century, when it was introduced by Stanislaus Mink von Wennsshein. Von Wennsshein's basic construction was modified in the early eighteenth century by Dr Richard Grey, an Englishman. The Major System was devised to enable the master memorisers of the time to break the bonds of the previously excellent but more limited systems. These master memorisers wanted a system that would enable them to memorise a list of items not only longer than ten but as long as they wanted. At the same time they wanted this system to enable them to remember numbers and dates and to order and structure memory in hundreds and thousands of detailed ways.

The basic concept of the system is that it makes use of a different consonant or consonant sound for each number from 0 to 9 in a special code:

THE MAJOR SYSTEM'S SPECIAL CODE

Number		associated code
0	=	s, z, soft c
1	=	d, t, th
2	=	n
3	=	m
4	=	r
5	=	l
6	=	j, sh, soft ch, dg, soft g
7	=	k, hard ch, hard c, hard g, ng, qu
8	=	f, v
9	=	b, p

The vowels *a, e, i, o, u* and the letters *h, w* and *y* do not have numbers associated with them and are used simply as 'blanks' in the Key Memory Image Words you will soon be creating.

To save you the trouble of remembering these by rote, there are some simple remembering devices:

0 The letter *s*, or *z*, is the first sound of the word *zero; o* is the last letter.

1 The letters *d* and *t* have one downstroke.

2 The letter *n* has two downstrokes.

3 The letter *m* has three downstrokes.

4 The letter *r* is the last letter in the word *four*.

5 The letter *l* can be thought of as either the Roman numeral for 50 or a hand with five spread fingers, the index finger and thumb forming an L shape.

6 The letter *j* is the mirror image of 6.

7 The letter *k*, when seen as a capital, contains two number 7s.

8 The letter *f*, when handwritten, has two loops, similar to the number 8.

9 The letters *b* and *p* are the mirror image of 9.

As with the Number-Rhyme and Number-Shape Systems, your task is to create a Key Image Word that can be immediately and permanently linked with the number it represents. Take, for example, the number 1. You have to think of a Key Image Word that is a good visual image and that contains only *d, t* or *th* and a vowel sound. Examples include *day, tea, toe* and *the*. When recalling the word chosen for number 1, let us say *day*, you would know that it could represent only the number 1 because the consonant letter in the word represents no other number, and vowels do not count as numbers in this system.

Try another example: the number 34. In this case the number 3 is represented by the letter *m*, and 4 is represented by the letter *r*. Examples of possible words include *mare, more, moor* and *mire*. In selecting the 'best' word for this number, you once again make use of the alphabet order to assist both in choice of word and in recall: in other words, the letters you have to choose are *m* and *r*, so you simply mentally run through the vowels *a-e-i-o-u* using the *first* vowel that enables you to make an adequate Memory Word. The case in question is easily solved, since *a* fits between *m* and *r* to direct you toward the word *mare*.

The advantage of using this alphabet-order system is that, should a word in the Major System ever be forgotten, it can actually be 'worked out' from the basic information. All you have to do is place the letters of the number in their correct order and then 'slot in', in order, the vowels. As soon as you touch the correct combination, your Key Memory Image Word will immediately come to mind.

First, letting the letter *d* represent in each case the '1' of the number, try to complete the words for numbers 10 to 19, using the alphabet order system for these numbers, in the Initial Major System Exercise below.

Don't worry if this exercise proves a little difficult, because immediately following is a complete list of Memory Words for the numbers 1 to 100. Don't just accept them: check each one carefully, changing any that you find difficult to visualise or for which you have a better substitute.

INITIAL MAJOR SYSTEM EXERCISE

10 _____

11 _____

12 _____

13 _____

14 _____

15 _____

16 _____

17 _____

18 _____

19 _____

The Major System – Initial 100 Key Words

1 Day	37 Mac	73 Cameo	
2 Noah	38 Mafia	74 Car	
3 Ma	39 Map	75 Call	
4 Ra	40 Race	76 Cage	
5 Law	41 Rat	77 Cake	
6 Jaw	42 Rain	78 Café	
7 Key	43 Ram	79 Cab	
8 Fee	44 Rare	80 Face	
9 Bay	45 Rail	81 Fat	
10 Daze	46 Rash	82 Fan	
11 Dad	47 Rack	83 Fame	
12 Dan	48 Rafia	84 Far	
13 Dam	49 Rap	85 Fall	
14 Dare	50 Lace	86 Fish	
15 Dale	51 Lad	87 Fake	
16 Dash	52 Lane	88 Fife	
17 Deck	53 Lamb	89 Fab	
18 Daffy	54 Lair	90 Base	
19 Dab	55 Lily	91 Bat	
20 NASA	56 Lash	92 Ban	
21 Net	57 Lake	93 Bum	
22 Nan	58 Laugh	94 Bar	
23 Name	59 Lab	95 Ball	
24 Nero	60 Chase	96 Bash	
25 Nail	61 Chat	97 Back	
26 Nash	62 Chain	98 Beef	
27 Nag	63 Chime	99 Baby	
28 Navy	64 Chair	100 Daisies	
29 Nab	65 Chill		
30 Mace	66 Cha-cha		
31 Mat	67 Check		
32 Man	68 Chaff		
33 Ma'am	69 Chap		
34 Mare	70 Case		
35 Mail	71 Cat		
36 Mash	72 Can		

You now possess the code and keys to a Peg Memory System for the numbers from 1 to 100 – a system that contains the pattern for its own memorisation. As you have seen, this system is basically limitless. In other words, now that you have letters for the numbers 0 to 9, it should be possible for you to devise Key Image Words for the numbers not only from 1 to 100 but also from 100 to 1000. This system could of course go on forever. For those of you who wish to do this, I have developed a system named SEM^3 (the Self-Enhancing Master Memory Matrix), which is outlined in detail in my book *Master Your Memory*.

An alternative method is to 'stick with' the method of making every number into a letter, and making a Key Memory Image Word from that combination of letters.

On the pages that follow I have devised a list of Key Image Words for the numbers 100 to 1000. After certain of the more difficult words I have included: (1) a suggestion for a way in which an image might be formed from the word; or (2) a dictionary definition of the word, the definition including words or ideas that should help you form your image; or (3) 'new' definitions for words that place them in a humorous or unusual but certainly more memorable form.

The remaining words are followed by blank spaces. In the space provided you should write in your own Key Words for, or ideas about, the image you will be using. In some cases, where the combination of letters makes the use of single words impossible, double words have been used, such as *no cash* for the number 276 (*n, hard c, sh*). In other cases it is necessary to include vowels (which have no numerical meaning) at the beginning of the word. For example, the number 394 (*m, p, r*) is represented by the word *empire*. In still other cases, words have been used of which the first three letters only pertain to the number. For example, the number 359 (*m, l, b*) is represented by the word *mailbag*. The final *g* is ignored.

If you wish to expand Your Major System beyond 100, your next task is to check this Major System list carefully. It would obviously be too much to ask you to do this at one sitting, so I suggest the more modest goal of checking, making images for, and remembering 100 items each day. As you go through the list, attempt to make your images of the words as solid as you can. Remember that as you memorise this entire list, you should try to use both sides of your cortex, making sure that you are reviewing and consolidating the order, while at the same time increasing and expanding your imagination, your creativity, and your awareness of your senses.

Even when words refer to ideas or concepts, bring them down to a more concrete level. For example, the number 368, represented by the Memory Words *much force*, should not be pictured as some vague power or energy in space but should be visualised as an image in which much force is used to accomplish or destroy – for example, a weight-lifter at the Olympics. In other words, in each case you will be attempting to make the Memory Word as pictorial and as memorable as possible. Remember the rules in chapter 5: exaggerate; move; substitute; be absurd; use colour.

In cases where words are similar in concept to previous words, it is most important to make your images as different as possible. The same caution applies to words that are pluralised because of the addition of s. In these cases, imagine a great number of items as opposed to one enormous item. You will find your consolidation of the words in the Major System useful not only because it will enable you to remember the astounding number of 1000 items (in order or randomly) but also because it will exercise your creative linking ability, which is so necessary for remembering anything.

A number of the words used as mnemonics in this Major System are interesting in their own right. As you check through and memorise each list of 100, have a dictionary by your side, for help if you run into difficulty selecting your Key Words. In these instances, it will serve as a means of solidifying the images for you, will enable you to select the best possible images or words, and will be of value in the improvement of your general vocabulary. If you have read my book *Speed (and Range) Reading*, combine, where feasible, the vocabulary exercises included in it with your exercises on the Major System.

100 Daisies
101 Dust
102 Design
103 Dismay
104 Desert
105 Dazzle
106 Discharge
107 Disc
108 Deceive
109 Despair
110 Dates – succulent, sticky fruit
111 Deadwood – decayed, often twisted, remains of trees
112 Deaden
113 Diadem – a crown; a wreath of leaves or flowers worn around the head

114 Daughter
115 Detail
116 Detach
117 Toothache
118 Dative – a noun case that expresses giving
119 Deathbed
120 Tennis
121 Dent
122 Denun – to take a nun or nuns away from a place or situation
123 Denim
124 Dinner
125 Downhill
126 Danish – native to Denmark
127 Dank – unpleasantly soaked or damp; marshy or swampy

128 Downfall
129 Danube – the river (or picture waltzing to the *Blue Danube*)
130 Demise
131 Domed – having a large, rounded summit, as a head or a church
132 Demon
133 Demimonde – the fringe of society
134 Demure
135 Dimly
136 Damage
137 Democracy
138 Dam full
139 Damp
140 Dress
141 Dart
142 Drain
143 Dram
144 Drawer
145 Drill
146 Dredge – apparatus for bringing up mud (or oysters) from the sea or river bottom
147 Drag
148 Drive
149 Drip
150 De luxe
151 Daylight
152 Delinquent
153 Dilemma – a position leaving a choice that is usually between two evils
154 Dealer
155 Delilah – temptress of Samson; false and wily woman
156 Deluge – a great flood; Noah's flood
157 Delicacy
158 Delphi – the ancient Greek town where the sanctuary

of the oracle was located
159 Tulip
160 Duchess
161 Dashed
162 Dudgeon – state of strong anger, resentment, or feeling of offence
163 Dutchman
164 Dodger – a wily, tricky, elusive person
165 Dash light – imagine the dash light in your car
166 Dishwasher
167 Dechoke – reverse the image of choke, either in relation to a car or to strangling someone
168 Dishevel – to make the hair or clothes loose, disordered, 'flung about'
169 Dish up – to serve food, usually applied to a slapdash manner
170 Decks
171 Decade
172 Token
173 Decamp – imagine confusion in the dismantling of tents, etc.
174 Decree – an order made by an authority demanding some kind of action
175 Ducal – imagine anything similar to or looking like a duke
176 Duckish
177 Decaying
178 Take-off
179 Decapitate
180 Deface
181 Defeat
182 Divan
183 Defame
184 Diver
185 Defile

186 Devotion

187 Edifying

188 Two frisky fillies – imagine them in a field or memorable enclosure

189 Two frightened boys – perhaps being chased by 188!

190 Debase – to lower in character, quality or value

191 Debate

192 Debone – to pick the bones out of, usually from fish

193 Whitebeam – a tree with long, silvery underleaves

194 Dipper – imagine a big dipper at a fairground

195 Dabble

196 Debauch

197 Dipping – imagine someone being dipped forcibly into water, as the medieval torture

198 Dab off – imagine a stain or blood being 'dabbed off' with cotton wool

199 Depip – to take the pips out of (imagine a pomegranate)

200 Nieces

201 Nasty

202 Insane

203 Noisome – harmful, noxious, ill-smelling

204 No Sir!

205 Nestle

206 Incision – a clean cutting of something, as with a doctor's scalpel

207 Nosegay – a small bunch of sweet-scented flowers

208 Unsafe

209 Newsboy

210 Notice

211 Needed

212 Indian

213 Anatomy

214 Nadir – the lowest point; place or time of great depression

215 Needle

216 Night watch

217 Antique

218 Native

219 Antibes – a port and resort in south-east France, on the Mediterranean

220 Ninnies – group of people with weak minds, simpletons

221 Ninth – imagine the ninth hole of a golf course

222 Ninon – a lightweight dress fabric made of silk

223 No name – imagine a person who has forgotten his name

224 Nunnery

225 Union hall

226 Nunnish – pertaining to or like a nun

227 Non-aqua – having nothing at all to do with water

228 Nineveh

229 Ninepin – one of nine upright pieces of wood to be knocked down in the game of ninepins

230 Names

231 Nomad

232 Nominee – a person nominated for a position or office

233 No ma'am

234 Enamour – to charm, to animate with love

235 Animal

236 No mash – imagine a saucepan that has just

been emptied of mashed
potatoes
237 Unmake
238 Nymph – a beautiful
mythological maiden,
always young
239 Numb
240 Nurse
241 Narrate
242 No run
243 Norm – a standard; a set
pattern to be maintained
244 Narrower
245 Nearly
246 Nourish
247 New York
248 Nerve
249 Nearby
250 Nails
251 Nailed
252 Nylon
253 New loam – freshly turned
rich and fertile soil
254 Kneeler
255 Nail hole
256 Knowledge
257 Nailing
258 Nullify
259 Nail-brush
260 Niches – vertical recesses
in a wall to contain a
statue
261 Unshod
262 Nation
263 Unjam
264 Injure
265 Unshell – to extract a
living organism from its
shell
266 Nosh shop – imagine a
corner snack-bar or
something similar
267 No joke – a joke that falls
flat
268 Unshaved

269 Unship – imagine a great
crowd of people being
ordered off a ship
270 Necks
271 Naked
272 Noggin – a small mug
and/or its contents
273 Income
274 Anchor
275 Nickel – a grey metal
related to cobalt
276 No cash – imagine
someone fumbling in his
pockets in order to pay a
restaurant bill
277 Knocking
278 Encave – to confine to a
dark place; to keep in a
cave
279 Uncap – imagine
schoolboys stealing one
another's caps
280 Nephews
281 Nevada
282 Uneven
283 Infamy
284 Never
285 Navel
286 Knavish – having the
characteristics of a
roguish trickster
287 Invoke – to address in
prayer; to implore
assistance or protection
288 Unfavourable
289 Enfeeble – to make
extremely weak and
unable to function
290 Nibs
291 Unpod – to take from the
pod, as peas
292 New pan – imagine a
brilliantly shiny frying pan
293 New beam – imagine the
first beam ever from the
sun

294 Neighbour
295 Nibble
296 Nippish
297 Unpack
298 Unpaved
299 Nabob – a wealthy person, especially one returned from India with a fortune
300 Moses
301 Mast
302 Mason
303 Museum
304 Miser
305 Missile
306 Massage
307 Mask
308 Massive
309 Mishap
310 Midas – the king who turned everything he touched to gold
311 Midday
312 Maiden
313 Madam
314 Motor
315 Medal
316 Modish – in the current style or fashion
317 Medic
318 Midwife
319 Mudpie
320 Manse – the home of a Presbyterian minister
321 Mend
322 Minion – favourite child, servant or animal; slave
323 Minim – a creature of the smallest size or importance; a musical note
324 Manner
325 Manila
326 Manage
327 Maniac

328 Manful – brave, resolute, bold
329 Monopoly – a popular board game
330 Maims
331 Mammoth
332 Mammon – the Syrian god of riches; worldly wealth
333 My mum
334 Memory
335 Mammal
336 My match
337 Mimic
338 Mummify – to preserve the body by embalming
339 Mump
340 Mars
341 Maraud – to make a plunderous raid; to go about pilfering
342 Marine
343 Miriam
344 Mirror
345 Moral
346 March
347 Mark
348 Morphia – the principal narcotic of opium
349 Marble
350 Males
351 Malt
352 Melon
353 Mile man – a man who runs a mile
354 Miller
355 Molehill
356 Mulish – imagine anything that is characteristic of a mule
357 Milk
358 Mollify – to soften, assuage, appease
359 Mailbag
360 Matches
361 Mashed

362 Machine

363 Mishmash – a jumble, hotchpotch, medley

364 Major

365 Mesh lock – imagine something like a gear cog meshing and locking or a lock that operates by an intricate mesh

366 Magician

367 Magic

368 Much force

369 Much bent

370 Mikes

371 Mocked

372 Mohican

373 Make muck

374 Maker

375 Meekly

376 My cash

377 Making

378 Make off – to hurry away, as a thief from the scene of a crime

379 Magpie

380 Mauve skirt

381 Mufti – an expounder of Mohammedan law; civilian dress as opposed to uniform

382 Muffin

383 Movement

384 Mayfair

385 Muffle

386 My fish

387 Mafeking – a town in South Africa, well known for relief of siege there in 1900

388 Mauve feet

389 Movable

390 Mopes – sulks; being dull or out of spirits

391 Moped

392 Embank – to confine or protect (river, road, etc.) by a bank

393 Wampum – name for money beads and shells used by North American Indians

394 Empire

395 Maple

396 Ambush

397 Impact

398 Mob violence

399 Imbibe – to drink in; absorb (often used of liquor)

400 Recess

401 Recite

402 Raisin

403 Résumé – a summing up; a condensed statement; a summary

404 Racer

405 Wrestle

406 Rose show

407 Risk

408 Receive

409 Rasp – to rub with a coarse file; to utter in a grating way

410 Raids

411 Radiate

412 Rattan – Indian climbing palm with a long, thin, pliable stem

413 Redeem

414 Radar – imagine 'beaming in' on some object in the sky

415 Rattle

416 Radish

417 Reading

418 Ratify – to settle, confirm, approve, establish

419 Rat bait

420 Reigns

421 Rained

422 Reunion

423 Uranium – a radioactive white metallic element

424 Runner

425 Runnel – a rivulet or gutter

426 Ranch

427 Rank

428 Run-off – a decisive final contest; a gutter or spillway

429 Rainbow

430 Remus – one of two brothers suckled by a wolf in infancy; he became one of the mythological founders of Rome

431 Rammed

432 Roman

433 Remember

434 Ramrod

435 Rommel – notorious German war leader

436 Rummage

437 Remake

438 Ramify – to form branches, subdivisions or offshoots

439 Ramp

440 Roars

441 Reared

442 Rareness

443 Rear man – the last man in a column or file

444 Rarer

445 Rarely

446 Raree show – a peep-show

447 Rearing

448 Rarefy – to lessen the density or solidity of, especially air

449 Rarebit – a dainty morsel; often applied to Welsh rarebit

450 Release

451 Railed

452 Reloan

453 Realm

454 Roller

455 Reel line – imagine a fishing line tangled on its reel

456 Relish

457 Relic

458 Relief

459 Relapse

460 Riches

461 Reached

462 Region

463 Regime – mode, style, diet; form of government

464 Rasher

465 Rachel

466 Rejudge

467 Raging

468 Arch foe – imagine yourself as a knight with one giant foe among a number of others

469 Reach up

470 Racks

471 Racket

472 Reckon

473 Requiem – a service spoken or sung for the peace of the soul of a dead person

474 Raker – imagine a man who does nothing but rake gardens

475 Recall

476 Roguish

477 Rococo – a highly ornamental, florid style in design

478 Recover

479 Rack up – colloquialism meaning to score points in sport

480 Refuse

481 Raft
482 Raven
483 Revamp – to renovate, revise or improve
484 Reefer – a marijuana cigarette
485 Raffle
486 Ravage
487 Revoke – a card player's failure to follow suit, though he could
488 Revive
489 Rough passage – a crossing over rough sea; a difficult or testing time
490 Rabies
491 Rabid – furious, violent, unreasoning, mad
492 Ribbon
493 Ripe melon
494 Rapier
495 Rabble
496 Rubbish
497 Rebuke
498 Rebuff
499 Republic – a society with equality among members
500 Lasses
501 Last
502 Lesson
503 Lyceum – a place in Athens where Aristotle taught
504 Laser – a superconcentrated beam of light coming from a vibrating substance
505 Lazily
506 Alsatian
507 Lacing
508 Lucifer
509 Lisp
510 Ladies
511 Lighted
512 Latin

513 Late meal
514 Ladder
515 Ladle
516 Old age
517 Leading
518 Old foe
519 Lead pipe
520 Lance
521 Land
522 Linen
523 Liniment
524 Linear
525 Lineal
526 Launch
527 Lank
528 Lunar flight
529 Line-up
530 Looms
531 Limit
532 Layman
533 Lame mare
534 Lamarck – famous French zoologist and botanist
535 Lamella – a thin plate, especially of tissue or bone
536 Lime juice
537 Looming
538 Lymph – a bodily fluid resembling plasma
539 Lamp
540 Layers
541 Lard
542 Learn
543 Alarm
544 Leerer
545 Laurel
546 Large
547 Lark
548 Larva
549 Larrup – colloquial for 'to thrash'
550 Lilies
551 Lilt
552 Lowland

553 Lilo mattress – a camping mattress that serves as a bed
554 Lowlier
555 Lily-livered
556 Low ledge
557 Lilac
558 Low life
559 Lullaby
560 Lashes
561 Legit – colloquial for that which is honest
562 Legion
563 Lush meadow
564 Lecher
565 Lushly
566 All-Jewish
567 Logic
568 Low shove
569 Lush pea
570 Lakes
571 Licked
572 Lagoon
573 Locum – colloquial for a deputy in any office, especially a doctor
574 Lacquer
575 Local
576 Luggage
577 Licking
578 Liquefy – to bring a solid or a gas to a liquid condition
579 Lock-up
580 Leaves
581 Livid
582 Elfin – like, or relating to, a fairy or an elf
583 Alluvium – soil deposited or washed down by the action of water
584 Lever
585 Level
586 Lavish
587 Leaving

588 Leave off
589 Lifeboat
590 Lips
591 Leaped
592 Lib now – imagine this phrase as a women's liberation placard
593 Low bum
594 Labour
595 Label
596 Lip chap – a cold sore on the lip
597 Lawbook
598 Leapfrog
599 Lap up
600 Chases
601 Chaste
602 Jason – and the Golden Fleece
603 Chessman
604 Chaser
605 Chisel
606 Cheese show
607 Chasing
608 Joseph
609 Cheese pie
610 Shades
611 Shaded
612 Showdown
613 Chatham – naval dockyard town on the River Medway, Kent
614 Chatter
615 Chattel
616 Chitchat
617 Cheating
618 Shadoof – a mechanism for raising water, consisting of a long pole hung from a post, and a bucket, used in Egypt
619 Chat up – to talk to a person of the opposite sex with further contact in mind

620 Chains
621 Chant
622 Genuine
623 Chinaman
624 Joiner
625 Channel
626 Change
627 Chink – in the armour
628 Geneva – headquarters for certain United Nations organisations; major city of Switzerland
629 Shinbone
630 Chums
631 Ashamed
632 Showman
633 Jemima – boot with elastic sides, having no laces or clasps to fasten
634 Chimera – a fire-breathing monster with a lion's head, a goat's body and a dragon's tail; a fanciful product of the imagination
635 Shameless
636 Jimjams – nervous fears; delirium tremens
637 Jamaica
638 Shameful
639 Champ
640 Cheers
641 Chart
642 Shrine
643 Chairman
644 Juror
645 Churl – a surly, ill-bred man
646 Charge
647 Cherokee – North American Indian
648 Giraffe
649 Chirp
650 Jealous
651 Child
652 Chilean

653 Shalom – salutation at meeting or parting, used by Jews
654 Jailer
655 Shallowly – in a manner not intellectual or lacking in depth
656 Geology
657 Gelignite
658 Shelf
659 Julep – with mint
660 Judges
661 Judged
662 Jejune – bare, meagre, empty; void of interest
663 Judgement
664 Judger
665 Jewishly
666 Choo-choo-choo – an especially puffy steam engine
667 Joshing – good-natured leg pulling or joking
668 Jehoshaphat – a king of Judah
669 Shoe shop
670 Checks
671 Checked
672 Chicken
673 Checkmate – a position in chess in which the opponent's king is trapped; the end of the game
674 Checker
675 Chuckle
676 Check shirt
677 Checking
678 Chekhov – famous Russian author of plays and short stories
679 Jacob
680 Chafes – makes sore or worn by rubbing; irritates
681 Shaft

682 Shaven
683 Chief Mohawk
684 Shaver
685 Joyful
686 Chiffchaff – small European warbler with yellowish-brown plumage
687 Chafing
688 Shove off
689 Shavable
690 Chaps
691 Chapter
692 Japan
693 Jobman
694 Chopper
695 Chapel
696 Sheepish
697 Chipping
698 Sheepfold
699 Shopboy
700 Kisses
701 Cast
702 Casino
703 Chasm
704 Kisser
705 Gazelle
706 Kiss-shy – reluctant to kiss
707 Cask
708 Cohesive – with the quality of sticking together
709 Cusp – the point at which two branches of a curve meet and stop; a pointed end, especially of a crescent moon
710 Cats
711 Cadet
712 Cotton
713 Gotham – a proverbially foolish town
714 Guitar
715 Cattle
716 Cottage
717 Coating
718 Cadaver – a corpse

719 Cut up
720 Cans
721 Canada
722 Cannon
723 Economy
724 Coiner
725 Kennel
726 Conjurer
727 Conk – colloquial for 'to bang on the head'
728 Convey
729 Canopy – a covering over a bed or a throne
730 Cameos – pieces of relief carving in stone and agate, etc., with colour layers utilised to give background
731 Comet
732 Common
733 Commemorate
734 Camera
735 Camel
736 Game show – as seen on television
737 Comic
738 Comfy
739 Camp
740 Caress
741 Card
742 Corn
743 Cram
744 Career
745 Carol
746 Crash
747 Crack
748 Carafe – a glass water or wine bottle for the dinner table
749 Carp – to find fault; a freshwater fish
750 Class
751 Clod
752 Clan
753 Clam

754 Clear
755 Galileo – Italian astronomer, mathematician and physicist
756 Clash
757 Clack
758 Cliff
759 Clap
760 Cages
761 Caged
762 Cushion
763 Cashmere – a rich fabric or shawl, originally made in Kashmir, India
764 Cashier
765 Cajole – to persuade or soothe by flattery, deceit, etc.
766 Quiche shop
767 Catching
768 Cageful
769 Ketchup – tomato sauce
770 Cakes
771 Cooked
772 Cocoon
773 Cucumber
774 Cooker
775 Cackle
776 Quick change – rapid change of costume by an actor, etc., to play another part
777 Cooking
778 Quickfire
779 Cock-up – colloquial for that which has been made a mess of
780 Cafés
781 Cave-dweller
782 Coffin
783 Caveman
784 Caviar
785 Cavil – to raise needless objection

786 Coffee shop
787 Caving
788 Cavafy – poet of Alexandria
789 Coffee-bean
790 Cabs
791 Cupid
792 Cabin
793 Cabman
794 Caper – to frolic, skip, or leap lightly, as a lamb; a small berry used for making pickles and condiments
795 Cable
796 Cabbage
797 Coping
798 Keep off
799 Cobweb
800 Faces
801 Fast
802 Pheasant
803 Face mole
804 Visor
805 Facile
806 Visage
807 Facing
808 Face value
809 Face up - colloquial for 'meet the brunt'; accept the challenge or consequences
810 Fates – the three Greek goddesses of destiny
811 Faded
812 Fatten
813 Fathom
814 Fetter
815 Fatal
816 Fattish
817 Fading
818 Fateful
819 Football
820 Fans
821 Faint

822 Finance

823 Venom

824 Fawner – an obsequious or sycophantic person; one who insincerely praises for reward

825 Final

826 Finish

827 Fawning – courting favour by cringing

828 Fanfare

829 Vain boy

830 Famous

831 Vomit

832 Famine

833 Fame-mad

834 Femur – the thigh-bone

835 Female

836 Famish

837 Foaming

838 Fumeful

839 Vamp – adventuress; woman who exploits men; unscrupulous flirt

840 Farce

841 Fort

842 Fern

843 Farm

844 Farrier – a man who shoes horses or treats them for disease

845 Frail

846 Fresh

847 Frock

848 Verify – establish the truth of, bear out, make good

849 Verb

850 False

851 Fault

852 Flan

853 Flame

854 Flare

855 Flail – wooden staff at the end of which a short heavy stick hangs swinging; used for threshing

856 Flash

857 Flake

858 Fluff

859 Flab

860 Fishes

861 Fished

862 Fashion

863 Fishmonger

864 Fisher

865 Facial

866 Fish shop

867 Fishing

868 Fish food

869 Fish bait

870 Focus

871 Faked

872 Fecund – fertile

873 Vacuum

874 Fakir – a Mohammedan or Hindu religious devotee

875 Fickle

876 Fake china

877 Faking

878 Havocful – 'filled' with devastation and destruction

879 Vagabond

880 Fifes

881 Vivid

882 Vivien – Leigh

883 Five a.m.

884 Fever

885 Favillous – consisting of, or pertaining to, ashes

886 Fifish – resembling or having the characteristics of a fife

887 Fifing

888 Vivify – give life to; enliven; animate

889 Viviparous – bringing forth live young rather than eggs

890 Fibs
891 Fibbed
892 Fabian – employing cautious strategy to wear out an enemy
893 Fob-maker
894 Fibre
895 Fable
896 Foppish
897 Fee back – imagine yourself receiving money you had paid for a product that was unsatisfactory
898 Few puffs – imagine someone trying to give up smoking
899 Fab boy – colloquialism for a young boy considered very attractive by girls
900 Basis
901 Pasta
902 Basin
903 Bosom
904 Bazaar
905 Puzzle
906 Beseech – to ask for earnestly; to entreat, supplicate or implore
907 Basic
908 Passive
909 Baseball
910 Beads
911 Bedded
912 Button
913 Bottom
914 Batter
915 Battle
916 Badge
917 Bedding
918 Beautify
919 Bad boy
920 Bans – curses; interdicts; prohibitions; sentences of outlawry
921 Band

922 Banana
923 Benumb – to make numb or torpid, insensible or powerless
924 Banner
925 Banal – trivial, trite, stale, commonplace
926 Banish
927 Bank
928 Banff – a holiday resort in north-east Scotland, in Grampian Region
929 Pin-up
930 Beams
931 Pomade – a scented ointment, originating from apples, for the hair
932 Bemoan – weep or express sorrow for or over; to lament or bewail
933 Beam-maker
934 Be merry
935 Pommel – a rounded knob, especially at the end of a sword-hilt
936 Bombshell
937 Beaming
938 Bumph – derogatory term for official documents, forms
939 Bump
940 Brass
941 Bread
942 Barn
943 Brim
944 Barrier
945 Barrel
946 Barge
947 Bark
948 Brief
949 Bribe
950 Blaze
951 Bald
952 Balloon
953 Blame

954 Boiler

955 Balliol – one of the Oxford colleges

956 Blush

957 Black

958 Bailiff – a king's representative in a district; agent or lord of a manor; officer under a sheriff

959 Bulb

960 Beaches

961 Budget

962 Passion

963 Pyjamas

964 Poacher – one who trespasses to steal game or fish; a vessel for poaching eggs

965 Bushel – an 8-gallon measure for grain and fruit

966 Push-chair

967 Bushwhacker – dweller in the backwoods

968 Bashful

969 Bishop

970 Bacchus – the Greek god of wine

971 Bucket

972 Bacon

973 Becalm – to still; to make quiet; delay through lack of wind, as a yacht

974 Baker

975 Buckle

976 Baggage

977 Backing – support, moral or physical; a web of strong material at the back of some woven fabric

978 Back off

979 Back up

980 Beehives

981 Buffet

982 Buffoon – a ludicrous figure; a droll clown

983 Pavement

984 Beaver

985 Baffle

986 Peevish – fretful or irritable

987 Bivouac – a temporary encampment without tents

988 Puffy face

989 Puff up

990 Babies

991 Puppet

992 Baboon

993 Pipe major

994 Paper

995 Babble

996 Baby show

997 Popgun

998 Pipeful

999 Pop-up – an automatic toaster; book with pages that rise when opened to give a three-dimensional effect

1000 These zoos

13 How to increase by 1000 per cent everything you have learned so far

It is possible, with ten quick leaps of your imagination, to create a memory system of 1000 from the basic 100 and a memory system of 10,000 from the basic 1000. You use a similar method to that explained in chapter 10, which is simply to coat, cover or colour sections of your Major System in different substances, etc. For example, to expand the basic 100 words to 1000, using this new Multiplier Method, you would adjust the sections of your Major System as follows:

100–199	In a block of ice
200–299	Covered in thick oil
300–399	In flames
400–499	Coloured a brilliant and pulsating purple
500–599	Made of beautiful velvet
600–699	Completely transparent
700–799	Smelling of your favourite fragrance
800–899	Placed in the middle of a busy road
900–1000	Floating on a single cloud in a beautiful, sunny, clear sky

To multiply each of these ten 100s by 1000, thus giving you a total of 10,000, you use the same technique again. For example, by using the colours of the rainbow, you can bathe each of your 1000s in a different colour. Similarly, you could give each 1000 a different vision, or a different sound, or a different smell, or a different taste, or a different touch, or a different sensation. In these instances, the choice is up to you, and should be based on whatever gives *you* the strongest memory impressions.

For those interested in pursuing these Super-Memory systems further, see my books *Master Your Memory* and *Memory Visions*. In these books, the Self-Enhancing Master Memory Matrix (SEM[3]) outlines a complete system of 10,000 memory hooks, as well as providing 'key data' from the fields of art, music, literature, languages, geography, history, science and astronomy.

As with all previous systems, practise the Major System privately and with friends. You can probably already begin to sense that the memorisation of books, the preparation for examinations, and the like, are becoming increasingly easy tasks. The applications of the Major System are almost as limitless as the System itself and later chapters in the book will show you how to apply it to the memorisation of cards, long numbers, telephone numbers, dates in history, birthdays and anniversaries, and information for examinations.

14 Card Memory System

Magicians and memory experts often amaze and amuse audiences with their ability to remember complete packs of cards in the order in which they were presented. They similarly astound their audiences by being able to rattle off, without any difficulty, the six or seven cards not mentioned when an incomplete 'pack' is randomly presented. Extraordinary as these feats may seem, they are not all that difficult and are usually quite straightforward – even though many people accuse the performer of having hidden assistants in the audience, marked cards, and a number of other tricks.

The secret of remembering a complete pack of cards is to attach your Key Memory Image for each card to the Major System you have learned. All that is necessary to create a Key Memory Image Word for each card is to know the first letter of the word for the suit as well as the number of the card in that suit. For example, all words for the club cards will begin with *c*; all words for the hearts with *h*; all words for the spades with *s*; and all the words for the diamonds with *d*. The second consonant for the card-word will be the consonant represented by the letter from the Major System.

Taking as an example the 5 of spades, you know that it must begin with *s* because it is a spade card, and that its last consonant must be *l* because it is the 5, and 5 in the Major System is represented by *l*. Without much difficulty you arrive at the word *sale*, which represents the 5 of spades. If you wish to devise a word for the 3 of diamonds, it must begin with *d* because it is the diamond suit, and its final consonant must be *m* because the number 3 is represented by *m* in the Major System. Filling in with the first vowel, you arrive at the word *dam*, which is your Image Word for the 3 of diamonds.

Following is a list of the cards and their Memory Image Words. A few of the variations will be explained after you have had a chance to familiarise yourself with the list.

Clubs	Diamonds
CA—Cat	DA—Day
C2—Can	D2—Dan
C3—Cameo	D3—Dam
C4—Car	D4—Dare
C5—Call	D5—Dale
C6—Cash	D6—Dash
C7—Cake	D7—Deck
C8—Café	D8—Daffy
C9—Cab	D9—Dab
C10—Case	D10—Daze
CJ—Cadet	DJ—Deadwood
CQ—Cotton	DQ—Deaden
CK—Club	DK—Diamond

Hearts	Spades
HA—Hat	SA—Sat
H2—Hen	S2—Sin
H3—Ham	S3—Sum
H4—Hair	S4—Sear
H5—Hail	S5—Sale
H6—Hash	S6—Sash
H7—Hag	S7—Sack
H8—Hoof	S8—Safe
H9—Hub	S9—Sap
H10—Haze	S10—Seas
HJ—Headed	SJ—Sated
HQ—Heathen	SQ—Satan
HK—Heart	SK—Spade

In this system, aces count as 1, and the jacks and queens as 11 and 12, and 10 counts as 0, and the king simply as the name of the suit in which he resides. The Memory Words for the clubs and diamonds are in many cases the same as those for the Major System words for the seventies and teens, but this need not concern you, since the two lists will never come into conflict.

How does the memory expert dazzle his audience? The answer is quite simple: whenever a card is called out, he associates that card with the appropriate number of his Major System.

If, for example, the first card called out were the 7 of diamonds you would associate the word *deck* with the first word of your Major System, which is *day*. You might imagine the entire deck of a boat being bathed in daylight, making sure that in your association you smelled, saw, heard, tasted and touched as much as you could. If the next card called were the ace of hearts, you would associate the word of this card – *hat* – with the second word of your Major System: *Noah*. You might imagine Noah standing on the ark, wearing a gigantic rain-hat onto which the Flood is pouring and splashing in the most tremendous volume. You could actually imagine yourself as Noah, feeling the chill of the water and hearing the splashing, etc. If the next card called were the queen of spades, you would associate the word for that card – *Satan* – with your third Major System word: *Ma*. You might imagine your mother in a titanic struggle with Satan in the burning fires of hell, using as much motion, rhythm, colour and sensuality as possible. Throughout the memorisation of a pack of cards using the Major System as the pegs on which to hang the 52 items, you can see that you are clearly using both the logical, analytical, sequential and numerical left side of your brain, and the imaginative, colourful, rhythmical and sensual right side of your brain. From these few examples, I hope you can see how easy it can be to memorise an entire pack of cards in whatever order they happen to be presented to you. It is a most impressive feat to be able to perform in front of your friends.

Your facility for remembering cards can be taken a step further. It is possible to have someone randomly read you the names of all the cards in the pack, leaving out any six or seven. Without much hesitation, you can name these cards. There are two ways of doing this. The first is to use a technique similar to that explained in chapter 5. Whenever a card is called out, you associate the Image Word for that card within a larger concept, such as the block of ice previously mentioned. When all the cards have been presented, you simply run down the list of card Memory Words, noting those words that are not connected with the larger Memory Concept. If the 4 of clubs had been called, you might have pictured a car sliding across the huge cube of ice or being trapped within it. You could hardly forget this image, but if the 4 of clubs had not been called, you would immediately remember that you had nothing to remember.

The other system for this kind of feat is to mutate, or change, in some way the card Memory Image Word if that card is called. For example, if the king of clubs was called and your image for this was a caveman-like club, you could imagine the club being broken in half. Or if the card called was the 2 of hearts and your normal image of this was a simple farm hen, you might imagine it with an extraordinarily large tail.

The systems described in this chapter are basic to the remembering of cards, but it does not take much to see that in the actual playing of card games, a Memory System such as this can be of enormous help. You have probably watched people repeating over and over to themselves the cards that they know have been put down or which are in other players' hands, and you have probably seen them sigh with exasperation at their inability to remember accurately.

With your new Memory System, such tasks will become easy and a joy, and whether you use it for serious card playing or simply for enjoyment, throughout the process you will be exercising your creative memory powers and increasing the usefulness of your brain.

15 Raising your IQ through the Long Number Memory System

The long number memory test on page 20 will probably have been particularly difficult (most people, in IQ tests, cannot remember numbers more than 7 or 8 digits in length). Given a long number such as 95862190377 to memorise, most people will try a variety of responses including: to repeat the build-up continually as the number is presented, eventually getting bogged down in the very repetition itself; to subdivide the number into two- or three-number groups, eventually losing both the order and content of these; to work out mathematical relationships between the numbers as they are presented, inevitably 'losing track'; or to 'picture' the number as it is presented, the picture becoming more and more blurred as the long number is presented.

If you think back to your own performance in the initial long number memory test, you will probably realise that your own approach was either one or a combination of those approaches just mentioned. Once again, the Major System comes to the rescue, making the task of memorising long numbers not only easy but enjoyable. Instead of using the Major System as a peg system for remembering lists of 100 or 1000, etc., you take advantage of its flexibility: going back to the basic code, and to the Basic Key Image Words you constructed for the numbers from 1 to 100, you use the Key Image Words in conjunction with the Link System to remember long numbers.

For example, take the number at the beginning of this chapter, 95862190377. It is composed, in sequence, of the following smaller numbers, each followed by its Major System Key Image Word:

95—Ball
86—Fish
21—Net
90—Base
37—Mac
7—Key

In order to remember this almost 'impossibly long' number, all you now have to do is to use the Basic Link System, making the words into a simple and imaginative little story. For example, you could imagine a brilliant, rainbow-coloured *ball* bouncing with a loud boing off the head of a gigantic and beautifully coloured *fish* that had just fought its way out of a very tangled and dripping-wet *net*, which was slowly collapsing to the *base* level of a pier, where it wrapped itself around a man, wearing a fawn-coloured and wind-blown *mac*, just as he was bending over to pick up the *key*, which had dropped onto the pier with a loud clang.

At the end of this paragraph close your eyes and re-envision the little story. Now, recalling the Key Image Words, transform them into the numbers, and you will get:

b—9
l—5
f—8
sh—6
n—2
t—1
b—9
s—0
m—3
c—7
k—7
95862190377

It is not essential to remember long numbers using only groups of two. It is just as easy, and sometimes even more easy, to consider the numbers in subgroups of three. Try this with the number 851429730584. It is composed of:

851—Fault
429—Rainbow
730—Cameos
584—Lever

In order to remember this number, which is even longer than the previous one, it is once again a matter of using your Basic Link System to make up a single little image story using your Basic Key Image Words. Using your right-brain imagination, you can imagine some gigantic universal force that could cause a break or a *fault* in beautiful and shimmering *rainbow*-coloured *cameos*, which were so heavy they needed a gigantic *lever* to move them. Once again, at the end of this paragraph, close your eyes and refilm the little image story on your inner screen. Now recall the words and, transforming them, you get:

f—8
l—5
t—1
r—4
n—2
b—9
c—7
m—3
s—0
l—5
v—8
r—4

851429730584

Another system for remembering long numbers, especially if you have not committed the Major System's Key Image Words to memory, is to improvise with the basic Major System Memory Code, making up 4-consonant words from the number you have to remember. For example, with a 16-digit number, such as 1582907191447620, you could make up the following 4-digit numbers and Key Image Words: 1582 – *telephone*, 9071 – *basket*, 9144 – *botherer*, 7620 – *cushions*.

Here you could imagine a loudly and melodically ringing red *telephone* being thrown in a long and graceful parabolic curve into a *basket*, where an annoying person (a *botherer*) is jammed bottom-down (as in comedy films), while other people are throwing multicoloured and multimaterialed *cushions* at him. Again, at the end of this paragraph close your eyes and imagine the story, then fill in the words and the numbers in the space below:

If you ever run into difficulty with the order of the words, you can resolve this simply by using, instead of the Link System, either the Number-Shape or the Number-Rhyme System. For example, using the original number at the beginning of this chapter, 95862190377, you would simply link *ball* to your Key Image for the number 1; *fish* to your Key Image for the number 2; *net* to your Key Image for the number 3; and so on.

You could also use both the Roman Room System and the Alphabet System, simply placing the words you had decoded from the long number either alphabetically or in your Roman Room. Decide which approach to the memorisation of long numbers is best for you. Then, to check on the amazing difference this method of number memorisation can make, go back to the original tests in chapter 2, and see just how easy those initial numbers were.

*Once you have mastered this skill, you will have not only improved your memory and your creative imagination even further, but will have **actually raised your IQ**. One subsection of Intelligence Quotient measurements involves the ability to remember numbers. Between 6 and 7 is the average person's limit; a score of 9 or more puts you, in that subsection of the test, in the IQ range of 150 and more.*

16 Telephone Number Memory System

Rather than being lodged in memory, most telephone numbers find themselves on scraps of paper in a limitless range of sizes, colours and shapes, in pockets, drawers, briefcases, and that general storehouse of frustration I call 'The Forgettory'.

Remembering turns out to be easier than forgetting, and once again it is the Major System that comes to the rescue in this situation. The procedure for remembering telephone numbers is to translate each digit of the number you have to remember into a letter from the basic code of the Major System. Using the letters you have transcribed, you make up catchy words and phrases that 'link you back' to both the number and the person.

For example, start with the ten people whose numbers you tried to remember in the initial test on page 20.

TELEPHONE NUMBERS

Your health-food shop	787-5953
Your tennis partner	640-7336
Your local weather bureau	691-0262
Your local newsagent	242-9111
Your local florist	725-8397
Your local garage	781-3702
Your local theatre	869-9521
Your local discothèque	644-1616
Your local community centre	457-8910
Your favourite restaurant	354-6350

The following examples are possible solutions to these ten telephone numbers.

Your local health-food shop: 787-5953. This translates into the letters *g f g - l b l m*. Your memory phrase, starting with each number's letters, could be: *Good Food Guides: heaLthy Body heaLthy Mind.* In your imagination you would visualise healthy owners of the shop, and the Greek ideal of *mens sana in corpore sano,* perhaps even visualising Olympic Games in which all the participants had bought their food from this health-food shop.

Your tennis partner: 640-7336. This translates into the letters *sh r s - c m m sh.* Your visual memory phrase here might be: *SHows Real Skill - Can Make Masterly SHots.* Again you should visualise your tennis partner making the statement come true.

Your local weather bureau: 691-0262. This translates to the letters: *sh p d - s n sh n.* Here, if you can imagine yourself as a sculptor of the sun, making it into various shapes, and therefore yourself as god of meteorology, you can use a very condensed phrase that includes *only* the letters that translate back into the number: *SHaPeD SuNSHiNe!*

Your local newsagent: 242-9111. This translates to the letters *n r n - p d t d.* Again, you can use the condensing technique, imagining your local newsagent shouting: *'News! Read News! - uPDaTeD!'*

Your local florist: 725-8397. This translates to the letters *g n l - f m b g.* Imagine yourself just having given a bouquet of beautiful flowers to the one you love and wanting to shout about it to the world: *'Good News Lovers! Flowers Make Beautiful Gifts!'*

Your local garage: 781-3702. This translates into the letters *c f t - m g s n.* Imagine your garage as super-efficient, turning around every car within a day and giving it back to its owner in a condition as perfect as when it came off the assembly line: *Cars Fixed Today! Made Good aS New.*

Your local theatre: 869-9521. This translates to the letters *f sh p - p l n t.* Imagine that your local theatre is putting on a number of plays by Shakespeare and that as you attend each of the plays you experience the entire gamut of emotion: *Finest SHakespearian Productions Produce Laughter aNd Tears.*

Your local discothèque: 644-1616. This translates to the letters *ch r r - d j d j.* The latter part needs no changing, so all you have to do in this particular number is to find a little phrase for the first three letters, which is conveniently: *CHanges Revolving Records - DJ! DJ!*

Your local community centre: 457-8910. This translates to the letters *r l c - f b d s.* Imagine the whole joint jumping: *Really Lively Community – Football! Badminton! Dances! Swimming!*

Your favourite restaurant: 354-6350. This translates to the letters *m l r - ch m l s.* Imagine your restaurant offering excellent cuisine at reasonable prices: *My Lovely Restaurant – CHarges Moderate; Luscious Selections.*

The examples given above are, of course, very particular, and it will now be up to you to apply the system outlined to the telephone numbers that are important for you to remember. In some cases, the combination of numbers may present a greater than usual difficulty, and appropriate phrases or words may be almost impossible to devise. In such cases, the solutions are still fairly simple. In the first case, you may make up inappropriate words out of the numbers you have to deal with, and then use the basic system, making absurd and exaggerated images to link with the person whose telephone number you are trying to remember. For example, if the telephone number of one of your friends whose hobby is golf is 491-4276, you would take the Major System Memory Words for 49 (*rap*), 142 (*drain*) and 76 (*cage*). Your image for remembering this number would be of your friend rapping loudly on the drain, which has bars like a cage, with his golf club.

Now that you have mastered the basics of the Telephone Number Memory System, it is essential that you associate and link it to your own life. Therefore, in the space provided, make a note of the names and telephone numbers of at least ten people or places you need to remember, and before reading the next chapter make sure you have your own ten numbers firmly pictured in your memory. As you form the images, remember the Memory Principles, realising that the more enjoyable, humorous and imaginative you make the exercise, the better your memory for those numbers will be.

MY TEN MOST IMPORTANT TELEPHONE NUMBERS

1 _____

2 _____

3 _____

4 _____

5 _____

6 _____

7 _____

8 _____

9 _____

10 _____

17 Memory System for Schedules and Appointments

As with telephone numbers, many people find appointments and schedules hard to remember. They use similar systems for coping with their problem, the most common, of course, being the daily appointment book. Unfortunately, many people don't always keep their appointment books with them. In this chapter two systems are introduced, the first of which is for immediate daily use, the second for remembering schedules and appointments for an entire week.

The first involves your basic Peg Systems. Simply equate the number in your system with the hour of your appointment. Since there are 24 hours in a day, you can either join shorter systems together, with an appropriate total of 24, or use the first 24 Peg Words in one of the larger systems.

Assume that you have the following appointments:

    7 – Early-morning group athletics practice
   10 – Dentist
    1 – Luncheon
    6 – Board meeting
   10 – Late film

At the beginning of the day, you run through the list and check for words with associations.

The time for your early-morning group athletics practice is 7.00 a.m., represented by the Major System Memory Word *key*. Imagine your entire team physically unlocking the door to super health with a big key.

At 10.00 a.m. (*daze*) you have an appointment with the dentist. Imagine him putting earphones on your head that play such soothing music that you are literally in a *daze*, unable to feel any pain. (What may be interesting in this example is the fact that if you imagine this particular situation, you may actually be able to reduce the pain!)

Your next appointment, at 1.00 p.m. (1300 hours), is for lunch. The Key Word here is *dam*. Imagine your luncheon table and luncheon guests, including yourself, sitting down for lunch at the top of an enormous *dam*, looking at the limpid lake on one side and the roaring waterfall on the other.

At 6.00 p.m. you have a board meeting. The Major System Memory Word for 18 (1800 hours) is *Daffy*. The association here is not difficult: imagine the confidential matters of your board meeting being discussed with Daffy Duck presiding.

Finally, you have an appointment at 10.00 p.m. (2200 hours) to see a late film. The Major System Memory Word is *nan*, so you can imagine going to the film with your grandmother, or if you like Indian food, imagine yourself eating the Indian bread (*nan*) throughout the film.

You can easily 'order' these five appointments, either by using the Link System to link the images you have just made or by simply placing each of the five images on your basic Number-Shape or Number-Rhyme System.

The second system for remembering schedules and appointments may be used for an entire week. Take Sunday as day 1 of the week and ascribe a number to each of the other days:

Sunday	1
Monday	2
Tuesday	3
Wednesday	4
Thursday	5
Friday	6
Saturday	7

Having given a number to the day, you treat the hours as they are treated in the first system discussed above, and as they appear in railway, shipping and airline timetables. The day is considered to have 24 hours, from 2400 (midnight) through 1.00 a.m. (0100), noon (1200), 1.00 p.m. (1300), and back to midnight (2400).

Thus, for any hour and day of the week a 2- or 3-digit number is formed – day first, hour second. All that is necessary is to translate the number into the word of a Major System list. Having arrived at the word, you link it with the appropriate appointment. For example, suppose you had an appointment to see a car you wanted to buy at 9.00 a.m. on Tuesday. Tuesday is represented by the number 3, which in the Major System translates to the letter *m*. The hour, 9, translates to the letters *b, p*. Referring to the basic list, you will see that the Key Word for Tuesday at 9.00 a.m. is *map*. To remember this appointment, you might imagine the car you are going to see as bursting through a giant map, wrapped in a giant map or driving across a giant map.

As another example, suppose you have an appointment for a guitar lesson at 5.00 p.m. (hour number 17) on a Thursday (day number 5). The number derived from Thursday at 5.00 p.m. is 517, the word for this being *leading*. To remember this, imagine yourself leading an entire orchestra with your solo guitar. Make sure your imagination is guided by the Memory Principles and that you can hear all the sounds, feel your guitar, see the orchestra and the audience, etc.

You may think this system a bit cumbersome because it requires a fairly thorough knowledge of the larger numbers in the Major System, but this reservation can be overcome by 'rotating' the hours of the day to suit those hours in which you have most appointments. If, for example, your day does not usually start until 10.00 a.m., then 10.00 a.m. can be considered number 1 in your appointment memory system. In this manner, the most important and often-used hours in your day will nearly always be represented by only 2-digit numbers, i.e., the numbers from 10 to 100 in the Major System. As with the daily schedule memory technique, you can 'order' your week's schedules by attaching the images, in order, to the Major System. For practical purposes, it is usually best to start on the Daily Memory System first, becoming skilled and familiar with it, and then move on to the Weekly Memory System.

18 Memory System for Dates in Our Century

When you have finished this chapter you will be able to give the correct day of the week for any date between the years 1900 and 2000!

Two systems may be used, the first of which is faster and simpler and applies to only one given year, whereas the second spans 100 years and is a little more difficult. These systems owe much to Harry Lorayne, a well-known North American memory expert. Using the first of these systems, assume that you wish to know the day for any given date in the year 1971. In order to accomplish what may sound like a rather considerable feat, all that is necessary is to remember the following number:

377426415375

'Impossible!' you might say, but once this system is explained you will see that it is in fact very clear and easy to operate. The individual digits of the 12-digit number represent the first Sunday for each month of the year 1971. The first Sunday in April, for example, falls on the fourth day of the month, the first Sunday in December falls on the fifth day of the month, and so on. Once you have remembered this number (if you have difficulty, refer back to the chapter on Long Number Memory) you will rapidly be able to calculate the day of the week for any date in the year.

It is best to explain this concept with examples, so let us assume that your birthday fell on 28 April, and that you wished to know what day the date represented. Taking the fourth digit from your Memory Number you would see that the first Sunday fell on the 4th. By the process of adding sevens to this initial Sunday date you rapidly calculate that the second Sunday of the month fell on the 11th (4 + 7 = 11); the third Sunday of the month fell on the 18th and the fourth Sunday fell on the 25th. Knowing this, you recite the remaining dates and the days of the week until you arrive at the date in question: 26 April = Monday; 27 April = Tuesday; 28 April =

Wednesday. So your birthday fell on a Wednesday in 1971.

Suppose you wish to know the final day of the year. The process is similar. Knowing that the first Sunday of the last month falls on the 5th day, you add the three sevens representing the following Sundays to arrive at Sunday 26th. Reciting the next few dates and days we get: 27th Monday; 28th Tuesday; 29th Wednesday; 30th Thursday; 31st (the last day of the year) – a Friday.

As you can see, this system can be applied to any year for which you may especially need to know the days for dates. All you have to do is to make up a Memory Number for the first Sunday or, for that matter, the first Monday, Tuesday, etc., of each month of the year; add sevens where appropriate to bring you near to the day in question; and recite to that day.

An interesting tip in making use of the Memory Number of one year with relation to surrounding years is that with each year the first date for the days at the beginning of the month goes down one, with the exception of leap years, when the extra day produces a jump of two for the following year. In the years 1969, 1970, 1971, for instance, the first Sunday for January fell respectively on the 5th, 4th and 3rd days of the month.

The second of the two systems to be introduced in this chapter is for calculating the day for any date from 1900 to 2000. It is necessary in this system to ascribe to each month a number that will always remain the same. The numbers for the months are as follows:

January	1	July	0
February	4	August	3
March	4	September	6
April	0	October	1
May	2	November	4
June	5	December	6

Some people suggest that these be remembered using associations such as January is the first month, the fourth letter in February is *r*, which represents 4, and so on, but I think that it is better to use the number:

144025036146

making the words *DRaweR, SNaiL, SMaSH* and *THRuSH*. These can be then be linked by imagining a drawer on which a snail's shell is smashed by a thrush. In this way the key numbers for the months can be remembered.

In addition to the key numbers for the months, the years themselves have key numbers, and I have listed them, from 1900 to 2000.

0	1	2	3	4	5	6
1900	1901	1902	1903	1909	1904	1905
1906	1907	1913	1908	1915	1910	1911
1917	1912	1919	1914	1920	1921	1916
1923	1918	1924	1925	1926	1927	1922
1928	1929	1930	1931	1937	1932	1933
1934	1935	1941	1936	1943	1938	1939
1945	1940	1947	1942	1948	1949	1944
1951	1946	1952	1953	1954	1955	1950
1956	1957	1958	1959	1965	1960	1961
1962	1963	1969	1964	1971	1966	1967
1973	1968	1975	1970	1976	1977	1972
1979	1974	1980	1981	1982	1983	1978
1984	1985	1986	1987	1993	1988	1989
1990	1991	1997	1992	1999	1994	1995
	1996		1998			2000

This system is not so easy to master, but with a little practice it can become almost second nature. The method is as follows: given the month, numerical date and the year, you add the number represented by the month key to the number of the date, and add this total to the key number representing the year in question. From the total you subtract all the sevens, and the remaining number represents the day in the week, taking Sunday as day 1. If the total is exactly divisible by 7, e.g. 28, subtract one less 7 (in this case $3 \times 7 = 21$ instead of $4 \times 7 = 28$).

In order to check this system, we will take a couple of examples. The day we will try to hunt down is 19 March 1969. Our key number for March is 4, which we must then add to the date in question, which is 19: $19 + 4 = 23$. To this total we must add the key number for the year 1969. Referring to the list we find that this is 2. Adding 2 to our previous total we arrive at $23 + 2 = 25$. Subtracting all the sevens from this ($3 \times 7 = 21$) we arrive at $25 - 21 = 4$. The day in question is consequently the 4th day of the week, which is a Wednesday. The second date is 23 August 1972. Our key number for August is 3, which we add to 23, giving 26. The key number for the year 1972 is 6, which added to 26 gives us 32. Subtracting all the sevens ($4 \times 7 = 28$) from 32 we arrive at 4. The 4th day of the week is a Wednesday, which is the day for 23 August 1972.

The only exception to this rule occurs in leap years, and then only in the months of January and February. Your calculations will be identical, but for these two months the day of the week will be one day earlier than the day you calculate. As with other systems, the best way to gain confidence with these two is to practise them. Start with the easier one, then graduate to the more advanced.

0	1	2	3	4	5	6	7	8
1900	1901	1902	1903	1904	1905	1906	1907	1908
1909	1910	1911	1912	1913	1914	1915	1916	1917
1918	1919	1920	1921	1922	1923	1924	1925	1926
1927	1928	1929	1930	1931	1932	1933	1934	1935
1936	1937	1938	1939	1940	1941	1942	1943	1944
1945	1946	1947	1948	1949	1950	1951	1952	1953
1954	1955	1956	1957	1958	1959	1960	1961	1962
1963	1964	1965	1966	1967	1968	1969	1970	1971
1972	1973	1974	1975	1976	1977	1978	1979	1980
1981	1982	1983	1984	1985	1986	1987	1988	1989
1990	1991	1992	1993	1994	1995	1996	1997	1998
2000								2090

This system is not so easy to master, but with a little practice it can become almost second nature. The method is as follows: given the month, numerical date and the year, you add the number represented by the month key to the number of the date, and add this total to the key number representing the year in question. From the total you subtract all the sevens, and the remaining number represents the day in the week, taking Sunday as day 1. If the total is exactly divisible by 7, e.g. 28, subtract one less than 7 (in this case 3 × 7 = 21 instead of 4 × 7 = 28).

In order to check this system, we will take a couple of examples. The day we will try to count down is 19 March 1960. Our key number for March is 4, which we must then add to the date in question, which is 19, 19 + 4 = 23. To this total we must add the key number for the year 1960. Referring to the list we find that this is 2. Adding 2 to our previous total we arrive at 23 + 2 = 25. Subtracting all the sevens from this (3 × 7 = 21) we arrive at 25 − 21 = 4. The day in question is consequently the 4th day of the week, which is a Wednesday. The second date is 23 August 1972. Our key number for August is 3, which we add to 23, giving 26. The key number for the year 1972 is 6, which added to 26 gives us 32. Subtracting all the sevens (4 × 7 = 28) from 32 we arrive at 4. The 4th day of the week is a Wednesday, which is the day for 23 August 1972.

The only exception to this rule occurs in leap years, and then only in the months of January and February. Your calculations will be identical, but for those two months the day of the week will be one day earlier than the day you calculate. As with other systems, the best way to gain confidence with these two is to practise them. Start with the easier one, then graduate to the more advanced

Plate I The Link System – imagination, exaggeration, absurdity, association, colour . . . *See pages 47 to 49*.

Plate II An example of the Roman Room System. *See pages 65 to 66.*

3 The signing of the Magna Carta in 1215 marked a new age of sense and reason. To remember this date, we can use the phrase *New Document – Liberalisation*.

4 The Russian Revolution of 1917 was an uprising of the people against what they considered oppression. They demanded greater equality in the form of communism. Our Memory Phrase: *People Demand Communism*.

5 Printing presses are often great rotating machines that churn out thousands of pages a minute. We can imagine a small version of this as the first printing press, in 1454, which can be remembered by the word *RoLleR*.

6 The Battle of Waterloo in 1815 was a triumph for Wellington but can be considered fatal for Napoleon. Once again we use a Memory Word rather than a Memory Phrase to remember the date: *FaTaL*.

7 The invention of the telescope by Hans Lippershey in 1608 changed the way in which man saw the sky. Our Memory Phrase: *CHanged Sky Focus*.

8 In 1905 Einstein's Theory of Relativity shed new light on the way in which matter and energy exist. His theory solved a number of puzzles that had occupied man but also gave rise to many more. Our Key Word: *PuZZLe*.

9 In the French Revolution in 1789 the king was ranged against the people. Hence, we can remember the date by *King Fights People*.

10 The American Declaration of Independence in 1776 marked in America a feeling of optimism and confidence in a new way of life. This can be encapsulated in the one word: *CoCKSure*.

19 Memory System for Important Historical Dates

The two systems you have just learned enable you to remember the day for any date in this century. The next system will assist you in the memorisation of significant dates in history. In chapter 2 one of the memory tests included a list of ten such dates. They were:

1 1666 Great Fire of London
2 1770 Beethoven's birthday
3 1215 Signing of Magna Carta
4 1917 Russian Revolution
5 1454 First printing press
6 1815 Battle of Waterloo
7 1608 Invention of the telescope
8 1905 Einstein's Theory of Relativity
9 1789 French Revolution
10 1776 American Declaration of Independence

The method for remembering these or any other such dates is simple; it is similar to the method for remembering telephone numbers. All you have to do is to make a word or string of words from the letters that represent the numbers of the date. In most cases, there is no point in including the 1 representing the thousand, since you know the approximate date in any case. Let us try this system on the dates above:

1 The Great Fire of London in 1666 practically destroyed the city, leaving it a heap of ashes. Our memory phrase for the date 1666 would thus be: *aSHes, aSHes, aSHes!* or *CHarred aSHes Generally.*

2 Beethoven is famous for many musical accomplishments, but perhaps his greatest achievement was the Ninth Symphony, in which he included a choir. His style of music made full use of the percussion instruments. Knowing this, remembering his birthday in 1770 becomes easy: *Crashing CHoral Symphony.*

Plate IV An example of dream memorisation showing the Key
Main Images. *See pages 175 to 176.*

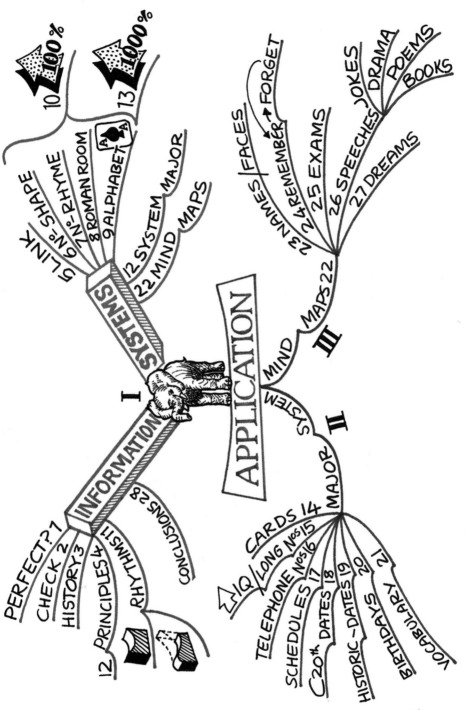

Plate III A Mind Map which summarises this book. *See pages 139 to 140.*

Remembering Birthdays, Anniversaries, and Days and Months of Historical Dates

The next system will be easy for you because it makes use of systems you have already learned. It is also easier than most other systems suggested for remembering such items because the large Memory System you have learned – the Major System – may be used as a 'key' for the months and days (other systems usually require code names that have to be especially devised for the months).

The system works as follows: months are assigned the numbers 1 to 12 and given the appropriate Key Word from the Major System.

January	day
February	Noah
March	Ma
April	Ra
May	law
June	jaw
July	key
August	fee
September	bay
October	daze
November	Dad
December	Dan

To remember a birthday, anniversary or historical date, all that is necessary is to form a linked image between the month- and day-words and the date you wish to remember. For example, your girlfriend's birthday falls on 17th June. The Key Word from the Major System for June is *jaw*; and the Key Word for 17 is *deck*. Imagine your girlfriend spending a deliriously happy day with you on the *deck* of a large boat, and the big *jaws* seeing your state of bliss, grins from ear to ear!

You wish to remember your parents' wedding anniversary, which falls on 25 February. The Key Word for February is *Noah*; and the

Key Word for 25 is *nail*. Imagine *Noah*, who 'married' the pairs of animals, trying to marry your parents by *nailing* them together!

Historical dates are just as easy to remember. For example, the date when the United Nations came into formal existence was 24 October. The Major System Key Word for October is *daze*; and the Key Word for 24 is *Nero*. Imagine a horse, *dazed* from the blaze caused by *Nero's* burning city, running into a situation where there is no strife.

To help you further in remembering birthdays, anniversaries, and the days and months of historical dates, it is useful to use a diary system such as the Universal Personal Organiser (UPO). (See page 181.) This system makes use of all the Memory Principles, and has specific sections devoted to enabling you to use Memory Systems for the memorisation of items such as that discussed in this chapter.

There is one small problem in this system, and this is the possibility of *knowing* the date but forgetting to remember it! This can be overcome by making a habit of checking through, on a regular basis, your memory links for the coming week or two. The memory system outlined in this chapter can be linked effectively with the previous system for remembering historical dates by year. In this way, you will have provided yourself with a *complete* date-remembering system.

21 Memory Systems for Vocabulary and Language

As mentioned in my books *Speed Reading* and *Master Your Memory,* vocabulary is considered to be the most important single factor not only in the development of efficient reading but also in academic and business success. This is not surprising when one realises that the size of one's vocabulary is usually an indication of the range of one's knowledge. Since vocabulary is the basic building block of language, it is desirable and necessary to develop methods of learning and remembering words more easily. One of the better ways of accomplishing this aim is to learn the prefixes (letters, syllables or words recurring before root words), the suffixes (letters, syllables or words recurring at the end of root words) and the roots (words from which other words are derived) that occur most frequently in the language you are attempting to learn. A comprehensive list of these appears in the vocabulary chapters of *Speed (and Range) Reading*.

Here are some more tips on how to improve your word memory:

1 Browse through a good dictionary, studying the ways in which the prefixes, suffixes and roots of the language are used. Whenever possible, use association to strengthen your recall.
2 Introduce a fixed number of new words into your vocabulary every day. New words are retained only if the principle of repetition, as explained earlier, is practised. Use your new words in context and as many times as possible after you have initially learned them.
3 Consciously *look* for new words in the language. This directing of your attention, known as mental set, leaves the 'hooks' of your memory more open to catch new linguistic fish!

These are general learning aids to assist your memory in acquiring knowledge of a language. They may be applied to English, as a means of improving your present vocabulary, or to any foreign languages you are beginning to learn. Having established a *general* foundation for learning words, let us be more specific in the remembering of *particular* words. As with other memory systems, the key word is *association*. In the context of language learning, it is well to associate sounds, images and similarities, using the fact that certain languages are grouped in 'families' and have words that are related.

To give you an idea of this linking method, I shall consider a few words from English, French, Latin and German. In English, you want to remember the word *vertigo*, which means 'dizziness' or 'giddiness', and in which a person feels as if surrounding objects were turning around. To imprint this word on the memory you associate the sound of it with the phrase *where to go?* which is the kind of question you would ask if you felt that all surrounding objects were rotating about you.

Two words that many people confuse in the English language are *acrophobia*, which is a morbid fear of heights, and *agoraphobia*, a mobid fear of open spaces. The distinction can be firmly established if you associate the *acro* in *acrophobia* with *acrobat* (a person who performs at a great height) and the *agora* in *agoraphobia* with *agriculture*, bringing to mind images of open fields (though the Greek word *agora* actually means 'marketplace').

Foreign languages are more approachable when one realises that they form groups. Practically all European languages (with the exception of Finnish, Hungarian and Basque) are part of the Indo-European group, and consequently they contain a number of words similar in both sound and meaning. For example, the words for *father*: German, *Vater*; Latin, *pater*; French, *père*; Italian and Spanish, *padre*. A knowledge of Latin is of enormous help in understanding all the Romance languages, in which many of the words are similar. The Latin word for *love* is *amor*. Related to *love* in the English language is the word *amorous*, which means 'inclined to love; in love; and of, or pertaining to, love'. The links are obvious. Similarly, you have the Latin word for *God: Deus*. In English, the words *deity* and *deify* mean, respectively, 'divine status; a god; the Creator' and 'to make a god of'.

French was derived from the speech of the Roman legionnaires, who called the head *testa*, hence *tête*, and the arm *brachium*, hence *bras*, etc. About 50 per cent of ordinary English speech is derived from Latin (plus Greek) either directly or by way of Norman French, leading to many direct similarities between French and English.

In addition to similarities based on language grouping, foreign words can be remembered in a manner not unlike that explained for remembering English words. Since we are discussing French, the following two examples are appropriate: in French, the word for *book* is *livre*. This can be remembered more readily if you think of the first four letters of the word *library*, which is a place where books are classified and studied. The French word for *pen* is *plume*, which in

English refers to a bird's feather, especially a large one used for ornament. This immediately brings to the mind the quill pen used widely before the invention of the steel nib, fountain pen and ball-point pen. The link-chain *plume – feather – quill – pen* will make remembering the French word a simple task.

Apart from Latin, Greek and French, the rest of English is largely Anglo-Saxon, going back to German, giving rise to countless words that are the same in German and English – *will, hand, arm, bank, halt, wolf*, etc., whereas others are closely related: *light (Licht), night (Nacht), book (Buch), stick (Stock), ship (Schiff)* and *house (Haus)*.

Learning languages, both our own and those of other people, need not be the frustrating and depressing experience it so often is. It is simply a matter of organising the information you want to learn in such a way as to enable your memory to 'hook on' to every available scrap of information.

One way to get a head start in learning is to realise that in most languages, 50 per cent of all conversation is made up of only 100 words. If you apply the Major System to the memorisation of these you are already 50 per cent of the way toward being able to understand the basic conversation of any native speaker.

For your convenience, the 100 basic words in the English language are listed overleaf. You will find that if you compare them with their counterparts in, say, French, German, Swedish, Italian, Spanish, Portuguese, Russian, Chinese, Japanese and Esperanto, nearly 50 per cent of these are almost the same as in English, with only minor variations in the accent and accentuation of the words. These translations are provided for you in *Master Your Memory*.

THE 100 BASIC WORDS THAT MAKE UP 50 PER CENT OF ALL CONVERSATION

1 a, an		**15** either/or	
2 after		**16** find (I find)	
3 again		**17** first	
4 all		**18** for	
5 almost		**19** friend	
6 also		**20** from	
7 always		**21** to go (I go)	
8 and		**22** good	
9 because		**23** goodbye	
10 before		**24** happy	
11 big		**25** have (I have)	
12 but		**26** he	
13 can (I can)		**27** hello	
14 come (I come)		**28** here	

29 how	65 she
30 I	66 so
31 I am	67 some
32 if	68 sometimes
33 in	69 still
34 know (I know)	70 such
35 last	71 tell (I tell)
36 like (I like)	72 thank you
37 little	73 that
38 love (I love)	74 the
39 make (I make)	75 their
40 many	76 them
41 me	77 then
42 more	78 there is, there are
43 most	79 they
44 much	80 thing
45 my	81 think (I think)
46 new	82 this
47 no	83 time
48 not	84 to
49 now	85 under
50 of	86 up
51 often	87 us
52 on	88 use (I use)
53 one	89 very
54 only	90 we
55 or	91 what
56 other	92 when
57 our	93 where
58 out	94 which
59 over	95 who
60 people	96 why
61 place	97 with
62 please	98 yes
63 same	99 you
64 see (I see)	100 your

Applying the Memory Principles to the memorisation of these words and others, you will find that language learning can be the easy, enjoyable task that most children find it to be. Children are no better at learning languages than adults; they simply open their minds more to the language and are not afraid to make mistakes. They repeat and make associations with the basics, listen more attentively, copy and mimic, and generally have a thoroughly good time without as much instruction as we adults think we need.

PART III: MIND MAPS FOR MEMORY

22 Mind Maps – Notes for Remembering

Most people forget what they note because they use only a tiny fraction of their brain in the note-taking process. Standard note-taking systems use sentences, phrases, lists and lines, and numbers. Such systems use only the left-cortex Memory Principles of order, sequence and number, leaving out imagination, association, exaggeration, contraction, absurdity, humour, colour, rhythm, the senses, sexuality and sensuality.

In order to make notes well, you have to break with tradition and use both the left and right sides of your cortex, as well as all the fundamental Memory Principles. In this system of note-taking, you use blank unlined pages, using a Key Memory Image (right brain) that summarises the central theme of the note you are making. From this central image you have a series of connecting lines (left cortex) on which are written (left cortex) or drawn (right cortex) the Key Image Words or actual images themselves of the main sub-areas and sub-themes you wish to note. Connected to these lines are more lines, again on which you place Key Image Words or Key Images themselves. In this way you build up a multidimensional, associative, imaginative and colourful **Mind Map** Memory Note of everything you wish to note.

Noting in this way, you will not only remember almost immediately and totally everything you write down because of the application of all the Memory Principles to this new multidimensional mnemonic note-taking approach but you will also find that the approach allows you to understand, analyse and think critically about whatever it is you are noting, while at the same time it gives you more time to pay attention to either the lecturer or the book from which you are learning. This technique and its applications are more fully outlined in my books *Use Both Sides of Your Brain* and *Make the Most of Your Mind*.

As an example, one of the editors responsible for revising this book used the **Mind Map** shown on Colour Plate III as a way of re-organising and summarising all the information contained in these chapters. A natural aggregation appeared: general information; specific systems; the Major Memory System and its application, and **Mind Maps** and their application.

Using Key Words and Key Images the **Mind Mapping** technique enables you to remember an entire book in one clear, single-sided, pictorial representation. The Memory and Creative Thinking Principles thus applied in your **Mind Map** notes enable you to tackle *any* new subject with ease and pass tests with 'flying colours'.

23 Remembering Names and Faces

Remembering names and faces is one of the most important aspects of our lives, and one of the most difficult. The reason for the difficulty lies in the fact that in most instances the names have no real 'connection' to the faces. In earlier ages it was exactly the opposite, and the whole system developed for giving people names was based on memory and association: the man you regularly saw covered in white flour with dough all over his hands was Mr Baker; the man you regularly saw in his own and everyone else's garden was Mr Gardener; the man who laboured all day over a hot fire pounding metal was Mr Blacksmith, and so on. As the generations changed and the family name became more and more removed from its original meaning, the task of the memorisation of names and faces became increasingly difficult, reaching the current situation in which the name is a word with no immediate associations with the face.

There are two major methods of coping with this situation, each method supporting the other. The first is the Buzan Social Etiquette Method; the second, the Mnemonic Method.

THE BUZAN SOCIAL ETIQUETTE METHOD FOR REMEMBERING NAMES AND FACES

The Buzan Social Etiquette Method for remembering names and faces guarantees that you will never again find yourself in a situation where you are introduced rapidly to five people and hurriedly repeated, 'Pleased to meet you, pleased to meet you, pleased to meet you, pleased to meet you, pleased to meet you,' having been introduced only to the five pairs of shoes at which you look in embarrassment because you know you are immediately going to forget all the names anyway (which you do!).

The Social Etiquette Method requires two simple things of you:

1 an **interest** in the people you meet
2 **politeness**

The method is the same as that which you might find described in a book of etiquette, yet even writers of etiquette books often fail to realise that the original rules were made not simply to enforce rigid disciplines but to allow people to interact on a friendly basis, the rules being structured formally only in order to enable the people to meet and *remember* one another. Select from the following Social Etiquette Memory Steps those that will most help you.

THE SOCIAL ETIQUETTE MEMORY STEPS

1 Mental set
Before you enter a situation in which you will meet people, mentally prepare yourself to succeed and *not* to fail. Many people enter such situations 'knowing' that they have a bad memory for names and faces and consequently set about proving it to themselves. If you 'know' that your memory is going to improve, you will notice immediate improvement. When preparing yourself for meeting people, try to make sure that you are as poised and relaxed as possible and, also, that wherever possible you have given yourself a two- to five-minute break for preparation.

2 Observe
When you are meeting people, make sure you look them straight in the eye. Don't shuffle around, with your eyes on the floor or looking into the distance. As you look at someone's face, be aware of the special facial characteristics, for this will help you also in the second mnemonic approach to the memorisation of names and faces. On pages 146 to 148 there is a 'guided tour' from the top of the head to the tip of the chin, enumerating the various characteristics and the ways in which they can be classified and typified. The more you become skilled at the art of observation, the more you will realise just how different one face is from another.

If you can sharpen your observational powers, you will have made a giant step toward the improvement of your memory. Blank looking, instead of real seeing, is one of the major causes for poor memory.

You can prepare your mind for this by 'exercising' your observational powers in public places. At different times give yourself different parts of the face to look at, so that on one day you might concentrate on noses, another day on eyebrows, another day on ears, another on general head shapes, etc. You will find to your surprise that each part of each face varies enormously from person to person, and that your increasing observation of the differences will help you to remember the new faces that you meet.

3 Listen
Consciously *listen*, paying attention as much as you possibly can to the sound of the name of the person to whom you are being introduced. This is a crucial stage of the introductory process, at which point many people fail because they were concentrating more on the fact that they were going to forget than on the sound of the name of the person to whom they were being introduced.

4 Request repetition
Even if you have heard the name fairly well, politely say something in the order of 'I'm sorry, would you mind repeating the name?' Repetition is an important memory aid; each repetition of any item you wish to learn greatly increases the probability of your remembering it.

5 Verify the pronunciation
Once you have been given the name, immediately confirm, by asking the person to whom the name belongs, if you have the correct pronunciation. This confirms your interest and once again repeats the name, increasing the probability of your remembering it.

6 Request the spelling
If there is any doubt about the spelling of the name, politely or playfully ask for the spelling, again confirming your interest and allowing another natural repetition of the name.

7 Your new hobby – derivations
With a natural enthusiasm, explain that one of your new hobbies is the background and derivation of names, and politely ask the person to whom you have been introduced if he or she knows anything about the history of his or her own family name. (Be sure you know the history of your own surname!) It may surprise you to know that on average 50 per cent of people not only know at least some part of the background of their families' nomenclature but most of them are enthusiastic about discussing it. Once again you will have confirmed your interest in the individual, as well as having laid the ground for more repetition.

8 Exchange cards
The Japanese have developed card-exchange as a major social function, realising how useful it is for memory. If you are really interested in remembering people's names, make sure you have a very presentable card to give them, and in most cases they will give you their own or write the details down for you.

9 Repetition in conversation

Carrying the principles of interest, politeness and repetition further, make sure that during conversations with people newly met you repeat their names wherever possible. This repetition helps to implant the name more firmly in your memory, and it is also socially more rewarding, for it involves the other person more intimately in the conversation. It is far more satisfying for them to hear you say, 'Yes, as Mary has just said . . .' than to hear you say, 'Yes, as she [as you point] has just said . . .'

10 Repeat internally

During any little pause in the conversation look analytically and with interest at the various people who are speaking and about whom others are speaking, repeating internally to yourself the names that by now will be becoming second nature to you.

11 Check during longer breaks

If you have gone to get a drink for someone or for yourself, or for any other reason are momentarily alone in a crowd, spend the time scanning everyone you have met, repeating to yourself their names, the spelling of their names, any background material you have gathered about the names, plus any other items of interest that have arisen during the conversation. In this way, you will be surrounding each name with associations, thus building up a mapped network in your own mind that will increase the probability of future recall. You will be positively using the process described in chapter 24, on re-remembering.

12 Repetition at parting

As you say farewell, make sure you use the name of the person to whom you are saying it. Thus, by this time you will have used both the primacy and recency time-aspects of memory as outlined in chapter 11, having consolidated both your initial and final moments during the 'learning period'.

13 Reviews

a *Mental*. When you have parted from the new people, quickly flash through your mind all the names and faces of those you have just met.

b *Photographs*. When possible (for example, at a party), get photographs (either the formal ones or informal ones) of the event.

c *Your names and faces memory diary*. If you are interested in becoming a real Master Memoriser of names, keep a special diary in which you quickly sketch and make a Mind Map (see chapter 22) of the faces of those you have met, the names that attach to them plus any other Key Image Word information. A diary system such as the Universal Personal Organiser (UPO) is useful for this exercise.

d *Personal card file*. Keep a card file, noting on each card the time, place and date at which you met the person concerned. Keeping these cards in Mind Map form, especially using image and colour, increases the value enormously.

e *Mind Mapping*. Keep a general Mind Map recording your specific successes, and the Memory Foundations and Principles that worked particularly well for you.

14 The Reversal Principle

Wherever possible, reverse the processes through which you have just been. For example, when being introduced, repeat your own name, give the spelling, and if it seems appropriate even give the background. Similarly, make sure you present, where appropriate, your personal card. Throughout conversations, if you are referring to yourself, use your own name. This will help others to remember you, as well as encouraging them to use their names rather than pronouns during the conversations. In addition to being more polite, this approach will make the entire conversation more personal, enjoyable and friendly.

15 Pace yourself

There is a tendency, because of the stress of the initial meeting situation, for everyone to rush through it. The great names-and-faces memorisers and the founders of social etiquette invariably take their time, making sure that they have said at least one personal thing to everyone whom they meet. The Queen is a good example.

16 Have fun

If you make the learning of names and faces a serious and *enjoyable* game, the right side of your brain will feel far more free and open to make the imaginative associations and connections necessary for good memory. Children have 'better memories' for names and faces than adults *not* because their minds are superior but simply because they naturally apply all the principles outlined in this book.

17 The Plus-one Principle

If you would normally remember only between two to five of 30 people you have newly met, as the average person would, give yourself the goal of *one more* than you would normally remember. This establishes in your mind the principle of success and does not place the unnecessary stress of your trying to be perfect first time out. Apply the Plus-one Principle each time you are in a new situation and your road to success in the memorisation of names and faces is guaranteed.

A useful exercise/game at this stage is to take the first letter of each of the 17 Etiquette Memory Steps, and to make a memorable anagram of that. Use all the Principles!

HEAD AND FACIAL CHARACTERISTICS

1 Head

You will usually first meet a person face-to-face, so before dealing with the rundown of separate characteristics, we will consider the head as a whole. Look for the general shape of the entire bone structure. You will find that this can be: a) large; b) medium; or c) small. And that within these three categories the following shapes can be found: a) square; b) rectangular; c) round; d) oval; e) triangular, with the base at the chin and the point at the scalp; f) triangular, with the base at the scalp and the point at the chin; g) broad; h) narrow; i) big-boned; or j) fine-boned.

Fairly early in your meeting, you may see the head from the side and will be surprised at how many different shapes heads seen from this view can take: a) square; b) rectangular; c) oval; d) broad; e) narrow; f) round; g) flat at the front; h) flat on top; i) flat at the back; j) domed at the back; k) face angled with jutting chin and slanted forehead; or l) face angled with receding chin and prominent forehead.

2 Hair

In earlier days, when hairstyles used to be more consistent and lasting, hair served as a better memory hook than it does now. The advent of dyes, sprays, wigs and almost infinitely varied styles makes identification by this feature a tricky business. Some of the more basic characteristics, however, can be listed as follows:

Men: a) thick; b) fine; c) wavy; d) straight; e) parted; f) receding; g) bald; h) cropped; i) medium; j) long; k) frizzy; and l) colour (only in notable cases).

Women: a) thick; b) thin; or c) fine. Because of the variability in women's hairstyles it is not advisable to try to remember them from this characteristic.

3 Forehead

Foreheads can generally be divided into the following categories: a) high; b) wide; c) narrow between hairline and eyebrows; d) narrow between temple and temple; e) smooth; f) lined horizontally; or g) lined vertically.

4 Eyebrows

a) thick; b) thin; c) long; d) short; e) meeting at the middle; f) spaced apart; g) flat; h) arched; i) winged; j) bushy; or k) tapered.

5 Eyelashes

a) thick; b) thin; c) long; d) short; e) curled; or f) straight.

6 Eyes

a) large; b) small; c) protruding; d) deep-set; e) close together;
f) spaced apart; g) slanted outward; h) slanted inward; i) coloured;
j) iris – entire circle seen; or k) iris – circle covered partly by upper
and/or lower lid. Attention may also be paid in some cases to the lid
above and the bag below the eye, both of which can be large or
small, smooth or wrinkled, puffy or firm.

7 Nose

When seen from the front: a) large; b) small; c) narrow; d) medium;
e) wide; or f) crooked. When seen from the side: a) straight; b) flat;
c) pointed; d) blunt; e) snub or upturned; f) Roman or aquiline;
g) Greek, forming straight line with forehead; or h) concave (caved
in). The base of the nose can also vary considerably in relation to the
nostrils: a) lower; b) level; or c) a little higher. The nostrils themselves can also vary: a) straight; b) curved down; c) flaring; d) wide;
e) narrow; or f) hairy.

8 Cheekbones

Cheekbones are often linked very closely with the characteristics of
the face when seen front-on, but the following three characteristics
are often worth noting: a) high; b) prominent; or c) obscured.

9 Ears

Ears are a part of the face that few people pay attention to, and yet
their individuality can be greater than any other feature. They may
be: a) large; b) small; c) gnarled; d) smooth; e) round; f) oblong;
g) triangular; h) flat against the head; i) protruding; j) hairy; k) large-
lobed; l) no lobe; or m) uneven. This feature is of course more appropriate as a memory hook with men than with women, because the
latter often cover their ears with hair.

10 Lips

a) long upper lip; b) short upper lip; c) small; d) thick (bee-stung);
e) wide; f) thin; g) upturned; h) downturned; i) Cupid's bow; j) well-
shaped; or k) ill-defined.

11 Chin

When seen straight-on, the chin may be: a) long; b) short;
c) pointed; d) square; e) round; f) double (or multiple); g) cleft; or
h) dimpled. When seen from the side, it will be: a) jutting;
b) straight; c) double (or multiple); or d) receding.

12 Skin

a) smooth; b) rough; c) dark; d) fair; e) blemished or marked in some
way; f) oily; g) dry; h) blotchy; i) doughy; j) wrinkled; k) furrowed;
l) coloured or suntanned; or m) freckled.

Other characteristics of faces, especially men's, include the various and varied growth of facial hair ranging from short sideburns to the full-blooded and face-concealing beard with moustache. There is no point in listing all the variations. It should suffice to note that these hirsute phenomena do exist, but that they, like hairstyles and colours, can change overnight.

THE MNEMONIC NAMES AND FACES MEMORY PRINCIPLES

The Mnemonic Principles for remembering names and faces are identical to those outlined in chapter 4, emphasising: (1) imagination, and (2) association. The steps are as follows:

1 Make sure you have a clear mental image of the person's name.
2 Make sure you can actually 'hear again' the sound of the person's name.
3 Very carefully examine the face of the person to whom you are being introduced, noting in detail the characteristics outlined on pages 146 to 148.
4 Look for facial characteristics that are unusual, extraordinary or unique.
5 Mentally reconstruct the person's face, using your imagination in the way that a cartoonist does to exaggerate any noteworthy features.
6 Associate, using your imagination, exaggeration and the general Memory Principles, any of the outstanding features with the name of the person.

The quickest and easiest way for you to learn the application of these principles is to put them immediately into practice. On the following pages I have doubled the number of faces and names you were asked to remember in the original test on pages 21 to 23. I have given suggestions on how you might apply the principles to remembering the names associated with five of the faces. Look carefully at them and at the remaining 15, remembering as many as you can, then test yourself on pages 154 to 157.

Memorisation of Faces

If you wanted, for example, to remember the names of the faces on pages 150 to 153, you would simply apply the techniques outlined – looking closely at the faces, finding some characteristics that you could imaginatively associate with the name, and then making your mnemonic image.

For example, *Mr Mapley* (No. 9) is easy to remember in that his face is deeply furrowed and lined, and that his hair is similarly laced with patterns – thus a map, leading to Mapley.

Mr Suzuki (No. 12) has particularly pronounced eyebrows, which you could imagine as the flamboyant handlebars of a Suzuki motorbike.

Ms Knight (No. 15) has hair that hangs – thus you might imagine her bending her head down from the top of a castle, with some valiant knight climbing up her tresses to rescue her.

Mr Burn (No. 19) has very close-cropped and dark hair. You might imagine that his face was a countryside and that his hair was the result of a gigantic bush or forest fire that had *burned* all the vegetation.

Ms Hammond (No. 20), although she looks like the typical 'blonde beauty', also has a jowl structure that could remind you of the best leg of pork – ham!

One other point about remembering people: if you are *certain* that you will be meeting a person only once and are not concerned with your long-term memory of the name and the face, it is often useful to use an outstanding item of clothing that the person might be wearing. This method, of course, is no good for long-term memory, since a person will probably not be wearing the same clothes next time. The same point applies to hairstyles and beards.

Now check your memory of the faces and names you have linked, and fill in the names on pages 154 to 157.

1 Mr Mogambi

2 Mr Knorr

3 Ms Woodrowe

4 Mr Kokowski

5 Mrs Volkein

6 Mr Cliffe

7 Mr Momatt

8 Miss Ashton

9 Mr Mapley

10 Mr Dewhurst

11 Ms Jabanardi   **12** Mr Suzuki

13 Mr Welsh

14 Mr Macinnes   **15** Ms Knight

16 Ms Parsons

17 Ms Cook

18 Mr Pong

19 Mr Burn

20 Ms Hammond

16

6

12

9

19

4

15

11

18

10

3

8

14

17

7

5

2

1

20

13

As you establish your Social Etiquette and Mnemonic Memory techniques for names and faces, it is useful to have a Basic Image List of names you are likely to meet. In your Basic Image List simply have a standard image for common names that you can immediately link to the oustanding facial characteristic of anyone who has that name. Following is a list of examples that you can expand to fit your own social context:

Ashcroft the smouldering roof of a burned-out farm building with masses of flaky grey ash

Blake a gigantic, limpid blue lake in the shape of the letter *B*

Chalk the white cliffs of Dover

Delaney a giant ripping out country lanes (de-lane-ing)

Evans vans shaped like the capital letter *E*, the spine of the letter being the top of the van

Farren a tiny little bird (*wren*) seen at a phenomenally far distance

Goddard God with a 'hard' expression on his face

Humphrey a delighted prisoner humming a happy song as he is let out from behind the bars

Ivy ivy

King a Memory Principle throne

Lawrence Arabia!

Mercer someone pleading for and being given mercy

Nunn nun

Ovett imagine a veterinary surgeon swinging in a gigantic *O*

Patterson imagine the pitter-*patter* of your own son or the son of a friend as his little feet scurry across the ground

Quarry a gigantic and strong-coloured open-land mining area

Richardson picture in your mind the son of a 'rich, hard' father

Scott develop a symbol, such as kilt, haggis; anything typical, for you, of a Scottish person

Taylor make a suitable image

Underwood make sure the wood under which you place the image of the person is memorable, such as an old giant fallen tree

Villars a magnficent gleaming white Mediterranean villa

Wade imagine a person/animal wading thigh-high through a lake

Xanthou a standardised Memory Principle Image of 'Thank you'

Young a springtime image

Zimmermann an image of someone 'zimming' (like skimming/zooming) across the surface of water

Using the Etiquette Method, the Mnemonic Method and your standardised name/image system, you will now be well on the way to becoming a master in the memorisation of names and faces.

One more magic ingredient can be added to your ability, and it is summarised in an event that changed my life and that largely initiated my own interest in the art and science of memory. The event took place in the first class on the first day of my first year at my university. It was an eight-in-the-morning English lecture, and even the excitement of this first day had not quite managed to shake off the sleepiness in some of our heads. Our lecturer did. He strode into the room with no briefcase, no writing materials, no notes and no books, stood in front of the class, announced his name, and then said he would call the roll. Standing in front of the podium with his hands behind his back, he started calling out our names in alphabetical order, going through Adams, Alexander, Barlow and Bossy, in response to which he got the usual mumbled 'yes, sir' and 'here, sir'. When he came to Camburn, however, there was no reply. He paused for a moment and then said, 'Mr Barry Camburn.' There was still no reply. Without change of expression, he then said: 'Mr Barry Camburn, address 29 West Street, phone number 272-7376, born 24 June 1943, father's name Frank, mother's name Mary.' The only reply he got was the widening eyeballs and opened mouths of everyone else in the class. Our lecturer continued calling the roll, and every time he arrived at the name of a person who was absent, he called out the person's Christian name, address, telephone number, date of birth, and parents' names.

It was obvious to us that he could in no way have forelearned who was absent, and therefore he must have *all* of that data on *all of us* totally memorised. When he had completed the roll and everyone was sitting amazed, he repeated very rapidly the names of the students who were absent and said, with a wry smile on his face, 'I'll make a note of that sometime.'

Though he had never seen any of us, he managed to remember our names and our personal data in perfect order. Using the knowledge you gain from this book, see if you can work out how he did it, and when you have worked it out, apply it.

24 Re-remembering Remembering What You Have Forgotten

I recently sat down to a relaxed and delightful dinner with some business associates who included the newly elected president of a training and development organisation. He announced at the beginning of the meal that he had to get something off his chest or he'd explode: his car had just been broken into, the front windscreen smashed and his briefcase stolen. He was particularly frustrated because the briefcase contained his diary and a number of other items important to him.

As the pre-dinner drinks were downed, and the hors d'oeuvres completed, we began to notice that our friend was not really participating in the conversation and that he seemed to have a faraway look on his face as he very occasionally jotted notes on a scrap of paper. He eventually burst into the conversation again, announcing that he was ruining the evening for himself because he could remember only four items that had been contained in his stolen briefcase, that he knew there were many more, that he had to give a full report to the police within two hours, and that the more he tried to remember the more blocked he became.

Consider what *you* would have recommended that he do in order to recall.

Several of us at the table who were familiar with Memory Principles then took him through the following exercise: instead of continuing to allow him to concentrate on what he could not remember (what he in effect was doing was concentrating more and more on the *absence* of memory), we took him through what I call Reliving the Immediate Relevant Past. We asked him when he had last had his briefcase open. It turned out that it was at the office just before he left work, at which point he suddenly remembered that he had put two important magazine articles on the top of the pile in the briefcase. We then asked him when he had last had the briefcase open before leaving home for work. It turned out to have been the previous night after dinner, and he remembered having put in two more articles plus a tape recorder and a calculator, in preparation for the following morning. Finally we asked him to describe the interior design of his briefcase, and as he went through a detailed description of each compartment and section, he remembered pens, pencils, machines, letters and a number of other items that he had previously completely 'forgotten'.

Within 20 minutes of what turned out to be a delightful and playful reliving of his previous 24 hours, in which his frown gradually turned into a broad smile and his physical poise improved, he recalled 18 additional items to the original four he had recalled after a painful and unpleasant one hour and 20 minutes.

The secret in re-remembering is to allow the full power of your memory to flow freely without 'trying' to remember any one specific thing. The secret within the secret is to 'forget about' whatever it is you are trying to remember and to surround the absence (what you have forgotten) with every possible association or connection available to you (see diagram below). Usually the best way to do this is to 'relive' all experiences that connect in any way with the item you are trying to remember. This technique works immediately in practically all cases, and basically takes the form of an internally or externally created Mind Map around the 'absent' centre.

Forgotten 'Thing'

In those rare instances where there is not an immediate recall, complete the reliving exercise in exactly the way outlined, and then give your brain the instruction to forget about it on the conscious level but work it out on an unconscious level. You will find that within a few hours or days of this 'programming' you will suddenly be taken by surprise – at a meeting, while driving your car, in the shower, on going to sleep or waking, in the bathroom, etc., when your memory supplies the item you have forgotten. This memory technique, like the others, improves all other aspects of your memory as well as your creativity, and in addition gives you a special boost of confidence when you realise that, no matter what you have forgotten, you have within the left and right hemispheres of your brain an unconscious Sherlock Holmes who will solve any memory mystery you choose to give him!

25 Remembering for Examinations

You need no longer fear examinations:
- No more the year-long dread that increasingly looms like a storm on the approaching horizon as the year progresses.
- No longer the frantic, rushed, sweaty, frightening final few weeks' and days' build-up of tension before the event.
- No longer the stressful dash into the examination room in order to save every available second.
- No longer the nervous first rush through the examination paper, during which you read so fast that you have to read it again to find out what is actually being asked.
- No longer will you need to spend as much as 15 to 30 minutes of a one-hour examination jotting down random notes, scratching your head, frowning, frantically trying to recall all that you know and yet at the moment for some reason seem not to remember.
- No longer the frustration of not being able to dig out the essence from the mire of your generally disorganised knowledge.

The common scenario suggested above applies not only to those who know little about the subject but often to those who have a great deal of knowledge. I remember at least three students in my undergraduate years who knew more about certain subjects than practically everyone else in the year and who consequently used to give private tutoring and coaching to those who were struggling. Extraordinarily, these bright students would regularly fail to excel at examination time, invariably complaining that they had not had enough time in the examination room to gather together the mass of knowledge that they had and that for some reason they 'forgot' at critical moments.

All these problems can be overcome by preparing for examinations using the techniques for reading and studying outlined in *Use Both Sides of Your Brain* and *Speed Reading,* applying the Mind Map memory techniques as outlined in chapter 22 and especially by using the Major System in conjunction with the Link System.

Assume, for example, that the subject you wish to study and prepare to be examined in is psychology. As you study and organise your notes throughout the year, you would consciously and continually build up categories as demonstrated when remembering jokes (see page 171) that contain all the subcategories of the information.

In psychology these categories might include the following:

1 Major headings
2 Major theories
3 Important experiments
4 Significant lectures
5 Important books
6 Important papers
7 General significant points
8 Personal insights, thoughts and theories

Using the Major System you would allot a certain section to each of these major headings, attaching the Key Memory Image Words from your subjects to the appropriate Major System or Key Memory Image Word. For example, if you had devoted the numbers 30 to 50 to important psychological experiments, and the fifth of these was an experiment by the behavioural psychologist B. F. Skinner in which pigeons learned to peck for the reward of grain, you would imagine an enormous suit of armour (mail) taking the place of the skin (Skinner) of a giant and warriorlike pigeon who was pecking at the sun, causing millions of tons of grain to pour from heaven.

Using this approach, you will find it possible to contain an entire year's study within the numbers 1 to 100 and to transmit this organised and well-understood knowledge into flowing, first-class examination papers. If, for example, you were asked, in your psychology exam, to discuss motivation and learning with reference to behavioural psychology, you would pick the Key Words from the question and run them down your Major System Memory Matrix, pulling out any items that were in any way relevant to the question. Thus, the general form of your opening paragraph might be as follows:

In discussing the question of 'motivation and learning with reference to behavioural psychology', I wish to consider the following main areas of psychology: blank, blank, blank and blank; the following five theories: blank, blank, blank, blank and blank; the following three experiments, which support hypothesis A: blank, blank and blank; the following two experiments, which support hypothesis B: blank and blank; and the following five experiments, which support hypothesis C: blank, blank, blank, blank and blank.

In discussing the above, I wish to quote from the following books: blank, blank and blank; make reference to papers by blank, blank, blank, blank, blank and blank; include further references from course lectures given by blank on the following subjects: blank, blank, blank and blank; on the following dates: blank, blank, blank and blank.

And finally, in the conclusion of my answer, I will add a few of my own insights and thoughts in the following areas: blank, blank, blank and blank.

As you can see, you are already well on the way to a good grade, and at this stage you are still breezing through the introduction to your answer! It is worth emphasising that in any subject area the last category in your Memory System should be for your own creative and original ideas. It is in this category that the difference between first- and second-class examination results lies.

For a comprehensive coverage of how to prepare, read and study for exams, read the chapters in *Use Both Sides of Your Brain* on the Mind Map Organic Study Technique (MMOST), and for the application of this technique to family and business group study, read the appropriate chapters in *Make the Most of Your Mind* and *Harnessing the Para-Brain*.

Besides being able to remember information perfectly for examinations, by using the systems outlined in this book, you will also be cultivating the creative powers of your mind that lead to your complete success.

26 Memory System for Speeches, Jokes, Dramatic Parts, Poems, Articles and Books

SPEECHES

The best way to start approaching the memorisation of speeches to realise that in 90 per cent of cases they do not need to be completely memorised. Realisation of this fact will instantaneously help you overcome most of the major problems experienced by those who approach speech writing and speech making as a memory function:

1 The enormous amount of time wasted in preparing a speech for memorisation. The average time taken for the preparation and presentation of a one-hour speech is, in total, one week. This wasted time is spent writing and rewriting the speech again and again to make it appropriate for memorisation. The remainder of the wasted time is spent trying to ram the speech into the memory by constant repetition.

2 The mental pressure and stress caused.

3 The physical stress resulting from item 2.

4 The relatively stilted presentation that results from a word-for-word memorised presentation.

5 The boredom experienced by the audience who will 'sense' that what they are being given is lineally memorised and rigid, and not spontaneous and immediately relevant to them.

6 The aura of stress in both the speaker and the audience, both of whom wait with apprehension for those horrible gaps and pauses that occur when something has been forgotten.

7 The lack of eye contact between the speaker and the audience because the speaker is 'looking inward' at the rigidly memorised material and not outward to the audience.

The secret of making a good speech is not to remember the entire speech word for word, but the main Key Words of your speech. The entire process of preparation and memory/presentation can be made both enjoyable and easy if you follow these simple steps:

1 Research. Generally **research** the topic about which you are going to speak, making recordings of ideas, quotations and references that you think will prove relevant. These recordings should be done in the Mind Map form as basically outlined in chapter 22 and as expanded upon in *Use Both Sides of Your Brain.*

2 Mind Map – basic structure. Having completed your basic research, sit down and plan out, using a *Mind Map*, the basic structure of your presentation.

3 Mind Map – entire speech. With your basic structure in front of you, fill in any important details, still in **Mind Map** form, so that you have completed a left- and right-brain, associative, imagistic Mind Map Memory Note of the **entire speech**. Usually this will contain no more than 100 words.

4 Practise. Practise making your speech from this completed outline. You will find that, as you **practise**, the final order in which you wish to present the speech will become increasingly clear, and you can number the main areas and subtitles of your speech appropriately. You will also find that, having completed the research and thought in this way about the structure of the material, you will already have automatically memorised the bulk of your speech. Initially, of course, there will be points in it at which you will hesitate or get lost, but with a little practice you will find that you not only know your speech from beginning to end but know, at a much deeper level than most speakers, the real associations, connections and deeper structures of your speech. In other words, you will *really* know what you are talking about. This point is especially important, for it means that when you finally do speak to your audience, you will have no fear of forgetting the word order of what you are presenting. You will simply say what you have to say smoothly, using the vocabulary appropriate for the moment and not getting bogged down in a rigid succession of preordained sentence structures. You will thus become a creative and dynamic speaker.

An excellent book for those who wish to explore the art of presentation more fully is *Present Yourself* by Michael J. Gelb. In his book, Gelb bases his entire theory and approach on the Principles and information presented in *Use Both Sides of Your Brain* and *Use Your Perfect Memory.*

5 Peg Systems. As a backup safety system, you can always use one of the basic **Peg Systems.** Select the 10, 20 or 30 Key Words that completely summarise your speech and use the Memory Principles to connect your speech Key Words to the Peg System, thus guaranteeing that even if, for a moment, you do get lost, you will immediately be able to find yourself. Don't worry about any little pauses that might occur in your speech. When an audience senses that a speaker knows what he or she is talking about, a pause is actually more positive than negative, for it makes it obvious to the audience that the speaker is actually thinking and creating on the platform. This adds to the enjoyment of listening, for it makes the presentation far less formal and more personal and natural. Some great speakers actually use the pause as a technique, maintaining electrifying 'thinking silences' of up to as much as a full minute.

In those very rare instances when you do have to memorise an entire speech word for word, the process can be made easy by applying everything discussed so far in relation to speeches, and then, for the finishing touches, applying the techniques outlined in Dramatic Parts and Poems in this chapter.

JOKES

The problems and embarrassments associated with the memorisation and the telling of jokes are almost endless. In recent studies of business people and students, it was found that of the thousands of people questioned, nearly 80 per cent thought of themselves as not particularly good joke tellers, all wanted to be good joke tellers, and all listed memory as their major obstacle. The memorisation of jokes is actually far easier to deal with than the memorisation of speeches because the entire creative aspect of the work has already been done for you. The solution is in two parts: first, to establish a basic grid to categorise and capture the main element of the joke; and second, to remember the main details.

The first of these areas is easily dealt with by using a section of the Major System as a permanent library for the jokes you wish to file. First, divide the kind of jokes you wish to tell into general categories. For example:

> Sexual jokes
> Animal jokes
> National jokes (Irish, Japanese, etc.)
> Rhyming jokes
> Toilet jokes
> Kids' jokes
> 'Intellectual' jokes
> 'Saying' jokes
> Sport jokes, etc.

List these in numerical preference order and then devote sections of your Major System to these categories. For example, you might have the area from 1 to 10 or 1 to 20 for sexual jokes, the numbers from 10 to 20 or 20 to 40 for national jokes, and so on.

The second area is equally easy to handle: once again it involves your use of the Link System. Let us take, for example, the joke about the man who went into a pub and bought a pint of beer. Having been given his beer, he suddenly realised he had to make an urgent phone call, but he knew that some of the characters in the pub would swipe his pint before he returned. In order to prevent this, he wrote on the glass, 'I am the world's karate champion,' and went to make his telephone call, securely thinking that his beer was safe. When he returned, he immediately saw that his glass was empty, and he noticed more scribbling underneath his own. It read: 'Thanks for the pint – the world's fastest runner!'

To remember the joke, you consciously select Major Key Words from it, joining them to form the basic narrative. All you need from this entire joke are the Key Memory Words: 'pint', 'phone', 'karate champion' and 'running champion'.

To complete your memorisation, you imaginatively link the first Key Word to the appropriate Key Word in the Major System, and you use the Link System to connect the remaining three Key Memory Words. There are two major advantages to using this system: first, you will be able to remember clearly and categorise whatever jokes you wish; and second, the mass involvement of your right brain in the memorisation of the joke itself will make you a far more creative and imaginative joke *teller*, thus overcoming the second major problem for jokers, that of getting in a too rigid and linear, left-brained memorisation mode, which bores the listener.

DRAMATIC PARTS AND POEMS

For the university student, schoolchild and professional or amateur actor, this aspect of memory can be the most troublesome of all. The method usually recommended and employed is to read a line over and over again, 'get it'; read the next line, 'get it'; join the two together, 'get them'; read the next line and so on and so on ad nauseam until the first lines have been forgotten.

Systems based on the Memory Principles and used successfully by famous actors and actresses are the reverse. In this system the material to be remembered is read and reread quickly (see *Speed Reading*) and with understanding over a period of four days, approximately five to ten times per day. If you read for understanding continually in this way, you will become far more familiar with the material than you realise at the end of the twentieth reading, and you will be able to recall, without looking at the text, most of the material to be remembered. Your mind, especially if you have used your right-brain imagination to help you understand, will have absorbed practically 90 per cent of the information, and remembering will have become a natural outgrowth of proper reading and basic understanding using the tools of imagination and association.

This system is far more successful than the line-by-line repetition system, and it can be improved upon even further in the following way: once again you use Key Memory Words and the Link System. For example, if the material to be remembered is poetry, a few Key Words will help your mind 'fill in' the remaining word-gaps. If the material to be remembered is part of a script, once again the Key Image Words and Link Systems prove essential. The basic sub-divisions of a long speech can be strung together with Key-Word ease, and cues from speaker to speaker can be handled far more effectively if you imaginatively mnemonicise the quantum leap between the previous speaker's last word and your next word. It is lack of the use of these mnemonic techniques that often causes chaos on the stage, especially those long silences and breaks in continuity that occur when one performer forgets his last word or another forgets his first. Acting troupes can save as much as 50 per cent of their time, and thus enormously reduce stress and increase enjoyment and efficiency, by applying the Memory Principles to the theatrical works in which they are involved.

ARTICLES

You may need to remember the content of articles on a short-term or long-term basis, and the systems for remembering each are different. If you have to attend a meeting or make a brief résumé of an article you have only recently read, you can remember it almost totally, and at the same time can astound your listeners, by remembering the pages to which you are referring. The method is simple: take one, two or three Key Memory Image Words from each page of the article and slot them on to one of your Peg Memory Systems. If there is only one Key Image Word per page, you will know that when you are down to Key Image Word number 5 in your system, you are referring to the fifth page of the article, whereas if there are two ideas per page and you are at Memory Word 7, you will know you are at the top of page four.

For the memorisation of an article over a long period of time, it will be necessary for you to choose more than two or three Key Image Words per page and to use a more permanent Peg System in conjunction with the review programme as outlined in chapter 11.

BOOKS

It is possible to memorise, in detail, an entire book! You simply apply the memory techniques for articles to each page of the book you wish to remember. This is easily done using the Major and Link Systems in combination. Simply take one, two or three Key Memory

Image Words for page one and creatively link them to your Major System Memory Word for number 1: *day*. From page two you select another one, two or three Key Memory Image Words, creatively linking them to your number 2 Major System Key Memory Word: *Noah*, and so on. It will thus be possible for you, in a 300-page book, to remember not only what the basic content of each page was but, if you wish, what each section of each page contained.

MIND MAP METHOD

Another particularly effective method for memorising an entire book, article, dramatic part or poem, is the Mind Map method. Each chapter or section of the material you wish to memorise can be a branch of your Mind Map. If this is imaged and coloured, your brain will remember both the image and the colour, *and* the *position* of the branch on the 'clockface' of the Mind Map. Because the Mind Map uses all of your cortical skills, the probability of overall and particular memory is dramatically increased, as is the probability that if something should be forgotten, all the surrounding information on the Mind Map will 'pop up' the momentarily forgotten information.

27 Catching Your Dreams

Standard ability to remember dreams varies enormously from individual to individual. Some people, in fact, have such bad memories for their dreams that they sincerely believe that they are non-dreamers. This is not the case, for research during the past twenty years has shown that every human being has regular periods throughout the night during which dreaming takes place. This is evidenced by Rapid Eye Movement, in which the eyelids flicker and flutter, and occasionally the entire body twitches, as the body internally 'sees' and 'moves' with the imaginary story. If you have a cat or a dog, you may have noticed this kind of activity while it sleeps, for most higher mammals also dream.

The first step in the memorisation of your dreams is the actual retrieval of the dream itself. This you can accomplish by 'setting' your mind just before you go to sleep. As you begin to drift off, gently and firmly repeat to yourself 'I will remember my dream, I will remember my dream, I will remember my dream.' This will 'programme' your brain to give priority when you awake to the recall of the dream. It may take as many as three weeks before you 'catch' your first one, but the process is infallible.

Once you have caught a dream, you enter the second stage of dream memorisation. This is a tricky and 'dangerous' moment, for if you become too excited by the fact that you have actually caught one, you will lose it. This is because, for this type of memorisation, your brain needs to remain, for a while, in a *non-excited* state. You must learn to maintain an almost meditational calm, gently reviewing the main elements of the dream. You then very gently select two or three of the Key Main Images from the dream, and attach these, using the Memory Principles (which are dreamlike in themselves) through one of your basic Peg Systems.

Let's imagine, for example, that you had dreamed that you were an Eskimo stranded on an ice-floe at the North Pole and that you were writing, with gigantic felt-tipped pens, messages for help in the northern sky, forming multicoloured words that looked like the aurora borealis. For this you would need only two items from any Peg System. Take, for example, the Alphabet System. In this you would imagine that on the ice-floe with you was a gigantic and hairy *ape*, shivering exaggeratedly in the cold with you and thumping his chest to keep warm as an enormous *bee* buzzed in and out of the multicoloured images you were writing in the sky (see Colour Plate IV). Note that although the Alphabet System Image Word for the letter *A* suggested in chapter 9 is *ace*, it is permissible, as here, to use an alternative of your own choice.

Attaching the Major Dream Images to your Major Key Word System Memory Images in this way allows you to easily span the different brain-wave states in which you find yourself when asleep, when waking and when fully awake, thus enabling you to remember that important and very useful part of your subconscious life.

Numerous studies completed on people who have started to remember their dreams show that, over a period of months, they become more calm, more motivated, more colourful, more humorous, more imaginative, more creative, and far better able to remember. All of this is not surprising, for our unconscious dream world is a constant playground for the right side of the brain, where all of the Memory Principles are practised to perfection. Getting in touch with these at the conscious level encourages all connected skills to improve automatically.

If, as many people do, you become interested in this area of self-exploration and improvement, it is useful to keep a dream diary in Key Memory Word and Key Memory Image Mind Map form (see chapter 22). This diary will give you constant practice in all the skills mentioned and will become an increasingly useful tool in your overall self-development. After a little practice you may well find yourself both appreciating and creating literature and art at levels you had not previously explored. For example, Edgar Allan Poe first remembered and then used the more nightmarish of his dreams as the basis for his short horror stories. Similarly, Salvador Dali, the surrealist artist, publicly stated that many of his paintings were reproductions of perfectly remembered images from his dreams.

It should now be clear to you that the development of memory skills not only gives you the advantage of being able to remember more than you used to but also encourages the total development of the left and right hemispheres of your brain. This leads to a general expansion of memory powers, a burgeoning of your ability to create, and consequently a similar burgeoning of your capacity to appreciate the arts and sciences. It also enables you to understand yourself and the major areas of knowledge far more easily, and to contribute creatively to the storehouse of human creativity and knowledge.

Conclusion and Exercises for the Future

MEMORY-IMPROVEMENT EXERCISES

1 Start a programme of learning new subjects and new languages, in order to increase the basic memory store.

2 Encourage in yourself any activity that you have noticed helps you to remember.

3 Pay attention to your dreams, checking carefully the memory images which you thought you had 'previously forgotten'.

4 Occasionally attempt to 'take yourself back' to a period in your life, exploring *all* the elements of your life at that time.

5 Keep a diary using Key Words, special little drawings, as many colours as possible and Mind Maps. (The Universal Personal Organiser (UPO) is excellent for this – see page 181.)

6 Use the special Memory Systems and special Memory System Techniques for pleasure, for exercise, and for remembering.

7 Organise your learning time so that the primary and recency effects are maximised, and so that the sag-in-the-middle during learning is minimised.

8 Review, making sure that your review takes place just before the memory of what you want to remember starts to drop.

9 Encourage the use of your right cortical processes, as it is this side which provides you with the images and colour that make remembering easier.

10 Try to see and sense things in as much detail as possible – the more detail you store, the greater will be your ability to recall.

If you do this, and continue to remind yourself to remember by regularly referring to your books on memory, by leaving reminder notes in appropriate places, by devising review schedules, and by asking other people to do 'spot checks' with you, your mind and memory will provide you with increasingly improved performance for the rest of your life.

CONCLUSION

Now that you have completed *Use Your Perfect Memory,* you have started a giant mental engine running that will serve you for the rest of your life.

The more you practise the Memory Foundations and Principles, the more powerful your memory will become. The more powerful your memory becomes, the more your creativity grows. The more your memory and creativity grow, the more astute and honed becomes each of your senses.

You have therefore initiated a positive spiral of personal growth and development that will enable you not only to remember your dreams, but to make them come true.

An increasing number of people are beginning to follow the same path, and for your reference and enjoyment, the following pages include information on organisations, clubs, books, videos and other materials that will assist you in pursuing any of your personal development goals.

To your good and cherished memories!

Appendix

As you approach the end of *Use Your Perfect Memory,* I hope that you will be realising that it is not the end but the real beginning. With the physical beauty and complexity of your brain, and its enormous intellectual and emotional powers, with your ability to absorb information and to manage the memorisation of that information, and with the new techniques for allowing your brain to express and organise itself in matters which are more comprehensively attuned to the way you function, reading, studying, learning and life in general should become what they can be: delightful and flowing processes that bring not pain and frustration but pleasure and fulfilment.

Anyone interested in courses, products or further reading dealing with the subject covered in *Use Your Perfect Memory* can contact:

Buzan Centres   **(800) Y MIND MAP**
415 Federal Highway   **FAX: (407) 845-3210**
Lake Park, FL 33403
(407) 881-0188

1. THE BRAIN CLUB

The Brain Club is an international organisation designed to help you increase your mental, physical and spiritual awareness. This is done by waking that sleeping giant, your Brain, and teaching you how to access its vast intelligences, first by Learning How to Learn and then by developing specific skills in areas that you choose.

You can do this by studying in your own home, or meeting regularly with others who also wish to expand their vast range of mental skills as outlined in *Use Your Perfect Memory.*

Join these 'mental gymnasiums' and improve the following skill areas:

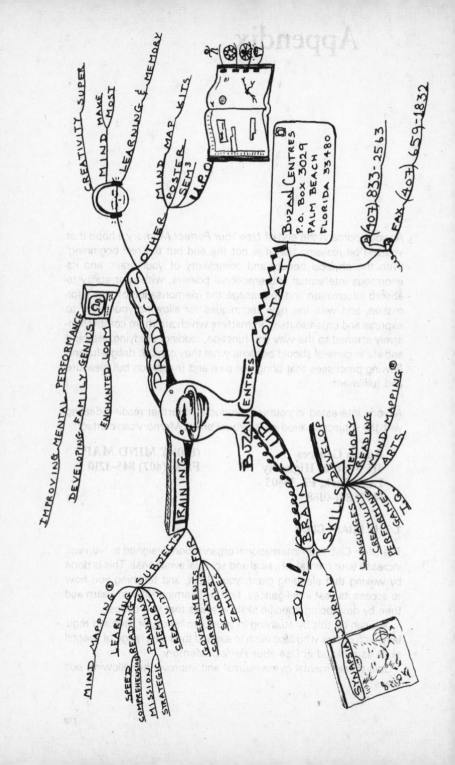

a Memorising
b Range/Speed Reading
c Mind Mapping
d Creative Thinking
e Learning and Studying
f IQ
g Mathematics
h The Arts
i Physical performance
j Vocabulary Building/Language Learning
k Communicating
l Personality Development
m Game skills
n Specialist skills

Each skill area within The Brain Club will be graded and certificates awarded as you reach advancing levels of competence. For details about The Brain Club, please contact The Buzan Centre, Inc.

2. PRODUCTS

The Buzan Centre offers many products useful for expanding the brain's potential.

Audiotapes

Supercreativity and Mind Mapping—a comprehensive introduction to the workings of your brain, and the theory and use of Mind Mapping (with manualette by Tony Buzan).

Make the Most of Your Mind—based on the book of the same name.

Learning and Memory—an interview with Tony Buzan, produced by *Psychology Today* magazine.

Videotapes

Improving Mental Performance—Buzan Business Training—three complete business training courses emphasising the application of Mind Mapping, Memory and Information Management to business.

The Enchanted Loom—documentary on the brain featuring interviews with the world's major contributors to the field, devised and presented by Tony Buzan.

Developing Family Genius—complete video series based in *Use Both Sides of Your Brain* and *Make the Most of Your Mind,* which guides the family through the latest information on the brain and learning how to learn.

Posters

'Body and Soul' poster—a limited edition poster depicting, in a surrealist manner, the principles taught by Tony Buzan. This beautiful picture is called 'Body and Soul' and each numbered copy is signed by the Swedish artist Ulf Ekberg.

Mind Map Kits

Specially designed Mind Map pads, with pens and highlighters.

Master Your Memory Matrix 0-10,000 (*SEM*[3])

Laminated 0–99 and 100 to 10,000 Matrix (*SEM*[3]) plus full instructions to assist the *Master Your Memory Reader*.

To order any of these products, please contact The Buzan Centre, Inc.

3. THE UNIVERSAL PERSONAL ORGANISER (UPO)

This *new* and *unique* approach to time and self management is a diary system, based on the techniques created and taught by Tony Buzan.

The Universal Personal Organiser is a living system that grows with you, and that provides a comprehensive perspective on your life, your desires, and your business and family functions.

The Universal Personal Organiser is the first diary system to use the principles that Leonardo da Vinci discovered in the Italian Renaissance: that images and colour enhance both *creativity* and *memory,* as well as being *easier* and more *enjoyable* than regular diary systems.

The Universal Personal Organiser *reflects you,* and gives you the *freedom* to perform at your highest potential. The Universal Personal Organiser is made of materials that are to the *highest quality,* using the best leathers and paper available.

The Universal Personal Organiser is designed to help you manage the four main areas of life: *health* (mental, physical and emotional); *family; creativity;* and *wealth.*

The Universal Personal Organiser, in so doing, allows you to organise your past, present and future in a manner that is both *enjoyable* and *fun.*

The Universal Personal Organiser's pages and partitions have been designed to enable you to get a comprehensive perspective on your *yearly plan,* your *monthly* and *weekly plans,* and your *daily plan,* using the new *24 hour diary clock, Mind Mapping,* and *Use Both Sides of Your Brain.*

4. BUZAN TRAINING COURSES

Courses are prepared for:
- ▶ Governments
- ▶ Corporations
- ▶ Schools and universities
- ▶ Private groups and organisations
- ▶ Foundations
- ▶ Children
- ▶ Families
- ▶ Senior citizens

The courses are based on the following books by Tony Buzan:
- ▶ *Use Both Sides of Your Brain*
- ▶ *Use Your Perfect Memory*
- ▶ *Make the Most of Your Mind*
- ▶ *Master Your Memory*
- ▶ *Speed Reading*
- ▶ *The Brain User's Guide*
- ▶ Universal Personal Organiser

The courses emphasise:
- ▶ Mind Mapping
- ▶ Memory skills—advanced
- ▶ Speed reading—advanced
- ▶ Planning
- ▶ Learning to read
- ▶ Creativity
- ▶ Presentation skills
- ▶ Work/study skills
- ▶ Corporate and family brain training
- ▶ The ageing brain
- ▶ Managing change
- ▶ Personal and time management
- ▶ Especially tailored courses

For enquiries, please contact The Buzan Centre, Inc.

5. FOR FURTHER INFORMATION ON:

► Training courses based on Tony Buzan's methods
► Co-ordination of The Brain Club
► Supportive books, tapes and educational products contact:

Buzan Centres   **(800) Y MIND MAP**
415 Federal Highway   **FAX: (407) 845-3210**
Lake Park, FL 33403
(407) 881-0188

Please send a stamped, self-addressed envelope for your reply.

ILLUSTRATION ACKNOWLEDGEMENTS
Black and white illustrations: A1 Creative Services; Nick Buchanan;
Mike Gilkes
Colour plates: Nick Buchanan

Bibliography

Atkinson, Richard C., and Shiffrin, Richard M. 'The Control of Short-term Memory.' *Scientific American*, August 1971.

Baddeley, Alan D. *The Psychology of Memory*. New York: Harper & Row, 1976.

Borges, Jorge L. *Fictions* (especially *Funes, the Memorious*). London: J. Calder, 1985.

Brown, Mark. *Memory Matters*. Newton Abbot: David & Charles, 1977.

Brown, R., and McNeil, D. 'The "Tip-of-the-Tongue" Phenomenon.' *Journal of Verbal Learning and Verbal Behavior* **5**, 325–37.

Buzan, Tony. *The Brain User's Guide*. New York: E. P. Dutton, 1983.

Buzan, Tony. *Make the Most of Your Mind*. London: Pan, 1988.

Buzan, Tony. *Master Your Memory*. Newton Abbot: David & Charles, 1988.

Buzan, Tony. *Memory Visions*. Newton Abbot: David & Charles, 1989.

Buzan, Tony. *Use Your Head*. London: BBC Books, 1989.

Buzan, Tony. *Speed (and Range) Reading*. David & Charles, 1988.

Ebbinghaus, H. *Über das Gedächtnis*. Leipzig: Duncker, 1885. op.

Gelb, Michael. *Present Yourself*. London: Aurum Press, 1988.

Haber, Ralph N. 'How We Remember What We See.' *Scientific American*, May 1970, 105.

Howe, J. A., and Godfrey, J. *Student Note-Taking as an Aid to Learning*. Exeter: Exeter University Teaching Services, 1977. op.

Howe, M. J. A. 'Using Students' Notes to Examine the Role of the Individual Learner in Acquiring Meaningful Subject Matter.' *Journal of Educational Research* **64**, 61–3.

Hunt, E., and Love, T. 'How Good Can Memory Be?' in *Coding Processes in Human Memory*, pp. 237–60, edited by A. W. Melton and E. Martin. Washington, DC: Winston/Wiley, 1972. op.

Hunter, I. M. L. 'An exceptional memory.' *British Journal of Psychology* **68**, 155–64, 1977.

Keves, Daniel. *The Minds of Billy Milligan*. New York: Random House, 1981; London: Bantam, 1982.

Loftus, E. F. *Eyewitness Testimony*. Cambridge, Mass.: Harvard University Press, 1980.

Luria, A. R. *The Mind of a Mnemonist*. Cambridge, Mass.: Harvard University Press, 1987.

Penfield, W., and Perot, P. 'The Brain's Record of Auditory and Visual Experience: A Final Summary and Discussion.' *Brain* **86,** 595–702.

Penfield, W., and Roberts, L. *Speech and Brain-Mechanisms*. Princeton, NJ: Princeton University Press, 1959. op.

Penry, J. *Looking at Faces and Remembering Them: A Guide to Facial Identification*. London: Elek Books, 1971. op.

Ruger, H. A., and Bussenius, C. E. *Memory*. New York: Teachers College Press, 1913. op.

Russell, Peter. *The Brain Book*. London: Routledge & Kegan Paul, 1966; Ark, 1984.

Standing, Lionel. 'Learning 10,000 Pictures.' *Quarterly Journal of Experimental Psychology* 25, pp. 207–22.

Stratton, George M. 'The Mnemonic Feat of the "Shass Pollak".' *Physiological Review* **24,** 244–7.

Suzuki, S. *Nurtured by love: a new approach to education*. New York: Exposition Press, 1969.

Thomas, E. J. 'The Variation of Memory with Time for Information Appearing During a Lecture.' *Studies in Adult Education*, April 1972, 57–62.

Tulving, E. 'The Effects of Presentation and Recall of Materials in Free-Recall Learning.' *Journal of Verbal Learning and Verbal Behaviour* **6,** 175–84.

von Restorff, H. 'Über die Wirkung von Bereichsbildungen im Spurenfeld.' *Psychologische Forschung* **18,** 299–342.

Wagner, D. 'Memories of Morocco: the influence of age, schooling and environment on memory.' *Cognitive Psychology* **10,** 1–28. 1978.

Yates, F. A. *The Art of Memory*. London: Routledge & Kegan Paul, 1966; Ark, 1984.

Index

age, memory and, 13, 14
alcohol, memory and, 13
Alphabet System, 69–74
anniversaries, remembering, 131–2
Anokhin, Pyotr, 16, 39
appointments, Memory System for, 121–3
Aristotle, 34, 36
articles, memorising, 173
association, 41, 42
Augustine, St, 35

birthdays, remembering, 131–2
Bohm, David, 38
Bonnet, Charles, 36
books, memorising, 173–4
brain:
    electrical stimulation, 38
    left-cortex functions, 39
    pattern-making ability, 16–17
    right-cortex functions, 39
brain cells:
    alcohol and, 13
    storage capacity, 16
Buzan Social Etiquette Method, 141–8, 158

Card Memory System, 109–12
card test, 21, 27
Cicero, 34
colour, 43

Dali, Salvador, 176
dates:
    appointments, 121–3
    birthdays, 131–2
    days of the week, 125–7
    historical, 129–30, 131–2
    test, 24, 30
days of the week, 125–7
deoxyribonucleic acid (DNA), 37
Descartes, René, 35
Diogenes, 33
DNA, see deoxyribonucleic acid
dramatic parts, memorising, 172–3
dreams, 15, 175–6
drink, memory and, 13

Ebbinghaus, Hermann, 37
eidetic memory, 17
exaggeration, 43
examinations, remembering for, 165–7
faces:
    characteristics of, 146–8
    Mnemonic Principles, 148–58
    remembering names and, 141–59
    tests, 21–3, 28–9, 148–57